ARTIFICIAL INTELLIGENCE

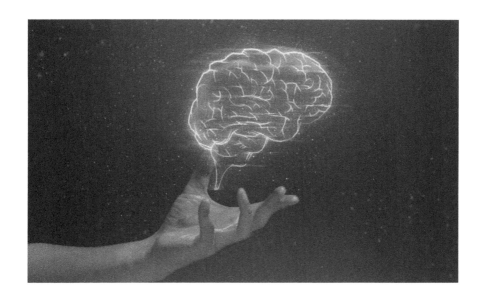

THE IMPACT OF THE EMOTIONAL STATUS
HEART BROKEN SYNDROME

NEUSA CORREIA LOPES

Library of Congress Control Number:		2024910513
ISBN:	Softcover	979-8-3694-2271-7
	eBook	979-8-3694-2272-4

Print information available on the last page.

Rev. date: 05/21/2024

To order additional copies of this book, contact:
Xlibris
844-714-8691
www.Xlibris.com
Orders@Xlibris.com
860374

CONTENTS

ACKNOWLEDGMENT

I dedicate this book to the world. To all students, educators and health care providers where technology and internet service seem to be lack of source. To my colleagues who work with lack of technology resources.

FOREWORD

Tick-tack, tick-tack. The heartbeat of the machines. The founder of the century-old Washington Post once said that a news story is the first scribble in history. A book, like this excellent essay by Neusa Correia Lopes, is "THE" beginning of history, which our grandchildren will probably tell their descendants about how they once had to go back to the times we live in today to understand their era.

In fact, this bold and portentous essay by Neusa Correia Lopes focuses above all on the present, for the present, anticipating the future that captivates and intimidates it. This work teaches us how to deal with the unknown from a purely technological point of view. It is also where the author's research comes from, with its impact on human health.

In fact, modern Artificial Intelligence systems have been developed by various companies away from the public eye. Until one of them, Open AI decided to open its own to anyone who wanted to test it in November 2022. That was Chat GPT. And the rest is history because it was a quantum leap.

As the capacity of these systems increases, so does the quality of delivery, dependency, and addition. From then on, the consequences are and will be unpredictable since, as other authors see it, we risk "losing control of our civilization." We are kicking the can down the road, saying hello to the Black Forest, which is the immeasurable power of machines.

While it is true that the development of technologies using Artificial Intelligence (AI) has created the idea that they can solve any problem, there are challenges and limitations. In the health sector, the tool contributes to faster and more accurate care and diagnoses, reducing costs and improving the experience of patients and professionals.

For example, the use of AI holds great promise for improving the speed and accuracy of disease diagnosis and screening, assisting in clinical care, and strengthening health research and drug development. According to the organization, AI can also support various public health actions, such as disease surveillance and systems management.

But what about its direct use by ordinary human beings? Well, that's the problem, and the author, after surveying specialists and various sources, tries and succeeds in assertively showing us how the unbridled, thoughtless, and chaotic use of technology has a direct link to the psycho-emotional state of each of us (often without us realizing it) and to various heart diseases. Heart rate, blood pressure, cardiac arrhythmia, and even strokes are pointed out here as possible consequences of electromagnetic radiation, radio waves, and frequencies that are harmful to human health.

Well, putting the brakes on technological development has been a vain effort since the invention of the wheel. If AI doesn't think up extermination plans on its own, which, for the time being, only exist in science fiction, this wheel will continue to turn, always forward. And with severe risks to human health.

Neusa Correia Lopes, skillfully and sagaciously, manages in this investigation to dive into the depths of the technological ocean that bathes the post-modern world to bring out a pinnacle of concerns that illuminate her already enlightened mind, which she reproduces, with thoughtful inflection and reflection, in this chapter book. Of course, there are pros and cons that Lopes sublimely lists in a work that she developed with the helpful and pertinent collaboration of the renowned Chinese visiting Scientist, Associate Professor Qiaoqing, currently residing in the USA, and which sprinkle this book with high notes of knowledge and scientificity.

The seriousness of this issue raises ethical questions because, at the end of the day, it focuses on human well-being. Governments around the world will have to realize this and synergistically seek to limit the risks intrinsic to the use of AI for health.

These principles should guide their work to support efforts and ensure that the full potential of AI for healthcare and public health is used for the benefit of all.

This is what Neusa Correia Lopes doesn't explicitly suggest, but what her work, with its captivating and easy-to-understand narrative, opens up over our heads, like an umbrella on a rainy day. In short, it's not every day that a literary work so forceful, so disturbing, so assertive falls on us because it's fruitful and largely verisimilar, as the magnificent researcher Neusa Correia Lopes has accustomed us to.

Herminio Silves

(Journalist-Director of Santiago Magazine Online Newspaper)

INTRODUCTION

In my previous book, educating our psycho-emotional and social state through the pandemic, I highlighted in my final chapters how teaching and learning may look in terms of structure, format, E-learning platforms, and logistics.

We all know that digital literacy has been with us for many years; however, now more than ever, there is a need for us to continue and force ourselves to learn more and discover what the digital world has to offer us.

Education nowadays is becoming a slave of artificial intelligence.

Digital literacy is what we need to input in our schools and community. Students, parents, and the community in general should benefit from its education. It is essential to be aware of digital literacy in depth.

I am expressing through this book my experiences, traveling outside the country in searching for changes in the digital world. How is artificial intelligence having its impact in today's world? Having said that, I believe that human beings are not capable of understanding AI's full potential and that it could threaten important factors in our world, such as careers and education. To challenge interpreters and comprehend the changes put by the AI, we need to manage our psycho –emotions and be aware of our social behavior. We feel that its power is using us.

Our emotions are part of our behavior. We need to be prepared emotionally in case of any chaos that could happen in our lives. People may most of the time ask: "Why do emotions trigger heart broken syndrome? This book alerts us that we should be aware of what we call "heart broken syndrome." This is a relevant health issue that Dr Qiaoqing Zong will have the opportunity to join me. She will address our emotions and the medical terminology about what Heart Broken Syndrome is. The impact that it will have on us. "Broken heart syndrome or heart broken syndrome," we also call Takotsubo Cardiomyopathy. Takotsubo cardiomyopathy is also known as stress-induced cardiomyopathy or broken heart syndrome.

So, can we say that we can relate the heart broken syndrome with education in terms of this new technology education realm?

We can sometimes or most of the time relate to it if we take into consideration the impact that this new teaching and learning use of technology is teaching us. The emotional impact of learning about new platforms and new technology routines. We are forced to learn new ways of teaching and learning now and soon, which makes us have lots of anxiety in the learning and in the teaching inputting process. We need to be careful with our emotions.

According to DR Qiaoqing Zong, "On the other hand, heart broken syndrome affects mostly the middle age and or the senior population. However, we cannot neglect the heart broken syndrome impact on the young population; (young people can also suffer from heart broken syndrome because of emotional stress or another kind of stress."

The new technology can easily impact the young population due to the fact that they are more vulnerable to the technology. For this reason, it is crucial to have control of the technology use among the youngsters.

How to prevent this emotional impact in terms of the new technology being used by this population?

The first thing to do is for this population to be ready to accept the changes, challenges, and accommodations that are confronting them.

Second, they must embrace the digital literacy of the new technology by seeing that it's convenient and practical.

Third is the emotional part of role-play as human beings. They need to know how to get out of their comfort zone and accept the new technology changes.

Furthermore, companies that make educational and health technology products should always follow up with the results and the impact of such technology being used by the population being served. Why? It is vital because after using the products, people can have either a negative or positive impact on them. So, companies should have surveys to improve their technological products for the future.

"Technology changes or improves as years come, and we can now see the velocity of its improvement. Teachers can offer important pedagogical insights for Ed-tech companies developing learning technology for students. Today, "teacherpreneurs" are sparking teacher-based technological innovation - and they're drawn largely from the ranks of the digitally literate. "Teacherpreneurs" are teachers who see the need for digital solutions in their classrooms, and some take on the roles where they coach other teachers on using technology external links as powerful differentiation tools."

https://rossieronline.usc.edu/blog/teacher-digital-literacy/

For example, years ago, we could press one to watch TV. Now, we can even talk to the TV to change the channels and have multiple channel choices.

CHAPTER – I

MY TRAVELLING AND THE DIGITAL REALM

During all my traveling, I have been thinking about the digital realm in education. It could be a good source that will help us find the invisible and prevent the world from getting another pandemic in the future. The reason for this picture is that we are still in the pandemic scenario. I can not talk about the digital realm without interrelating both scenarios.

The digital realm has become a concern for some people because it has threatened their jobs.

As I made my travels through Europe (Portugal), I found people worried about losing their jobs. The conversations that I heard in the coffee shops and supermarkets were about, "What are we going to do if robots take our jobs in a couple of years?" I hear the fear in their voices and the loss of their control as human beings threatened by a "robot." In schools, I heard parents talking about "What learning is going to be like?" Some think that learning is going to be difficult and that their children are not going to be able to adapt to this new learning style.

My way of thinking is that there is an urge to educate everybody on digital literacy. Even though this is not new for us. Indeed, there is a need for it. We have been dealing with technology for decades, but we have never gotten into a technological revolution like the one that we are living in. The pandemic urged us to use technology. This revolution is crucial; it is happening rapidly. Its velocity makes humans think and stress about what is going on in the world. However, I see it this way: the world just needs to adapt and accommodate this unique world of technological changes to avoid frustrations and emotional disorders.

Emotional needs to be in place and well managed so that our mind can deal with and recognize the new changes and try to adapt to them in a healthy mental way. Nowadays, we are in constant confrontation with AI robot machines, and technology changes everywhere in our daily lives. For instance, schools, supermarkets, coffee shops, banks, hospitals, airports etc. Below, I give some AI examples. We can replace human service with an AI service.

These are robots for you to pay for your purchase, and they will give you the change.

This robot checks in and makes reservations at hotels.

We need to be used to the next digital revolution. We cannot be afraid of it, in fact, we need to learn and explore ways to learn how to manage it in the future.

As we continue to go on with life, we notice the velocity of technology; for example, this year, in November 2023, I found Alice in Leiria, Portugal, at the municipal market, an AI cashier.

I report my experience with Alice; I went to buy some traditional cheese at the Municipal market, and in the end, I stopped paying and asked the owner, Mr. Fernando Gameiro, how much it was. He told me the amount to pay, and I gave him the money, and he said to me: "You have to pay Alice." I looked around, and I saw nobody. He laughed and said to me: "Alice is near you; just give her the money." I was shocked when he pointed to Alice, the AI. I laughed, and I inserted the money. Alice gave me change. Mr. Fernando Gameiro replied to me once again: "Alice is my cashier; she changes money, pays, charges, gives you the invoice, and has the cashier role. She does everything for me." MR Gameiro also told me that "Alice does not call sick or come late." For him, it is worthy to have an AI he reported to me. And he laughed when he also added to his comment, "I don't need to pay health insurance to

Alice." I found it clever! "As you can see, now we are changing humans for machines," I said; Wow! To myself, I can find AI now, even in the most vulnerable places. I had an encounter with "Alice," the AI cashier representative.

While walking in Boston at the train station on the floor, I found this BROWSE-BORROW-BOARD. Life becomes so easy as the digital world becomes crucial and interesting. It is true that I see a massive demand for digital education.

We can BROWSE for complimentary newspapers, magazines, and audiobooks to enjoy while you ride!

BORROW- these free e-books & magazines from the Boston Public Library – no library card required!

BOARD the T (train), and enjoy your free content! (the Mayor's office NEW URBAN MACHANICS).

This proves how important and interesting technology is becoming and how it is changing our behavior and our way of thinking. It shows us as well how rapidly it is going towards the new world in the future. Similarly, I say that we need to go with the flow and educate ourselves and our children on how to surpass this future to come. We must all be prepared for its changes and accommodation without retrograde, meaning no going back to the traditional in full. It is obvious that tradition will always exist. Thus, we can accomplish this with the existing new normal.

CHAPTER – II

DIGITAL LITERACY

Digital literacy has become a crucial issue to talk about around the world nowadays. This is the world of technology; it will allow us to have a faster and better understanding of what is surrounding our lives and not only that, but it also allows us to stay in different places at the same time when we try to use social media to talk about any project that we want the world to know about it. This velocity of having us human beings be at different places at the same time, talk to people from different countries, share our work, etc., makes us think about making adaptations and accommodations for the future world. The velocity of the technology is beyond our capacity to think. In fact, in order to control it, we need to be active in terms of acknowledging every step of technological development. According to Professor Arlindo Veiga, this is what he thinks: "Therefore, a greater focus on digital literacy is necessary. "We have a lot of room for improvement," assures professor Arlindo Veiga, who regrets the fact that many young people have "a Facebook account, an Instagram account, but then they don't know how to send an email and put the entire content of an email in the subject line. But I recognize that there are already young people who are taking advantage of this future that we have available."

We need to be able to understand its paradigm and think about where it is taking us. For this reason, we need to educate ourselves in digital literacy. As a matter of fact, Digital Literacy is related to the essential use of technology, such as the ability to produce digital content, the ability to use computers, network creation, etc. In addition, it improves digital equity among students, supports lifelong skills, and increases online security etc.

What is Digital Literacy?

"The term 'digital literacy' was coined in 1997 by Paul Glister, who defined it as "the ability to both understand and use digitized information" (Glister 1972). The concept, which had been discussed widely throughout the 1990s, was built upon the discourses of visual literacy (using non-textual symbols and images to make sense of knowledge), technological literacy (the ability to use a particular technology or technologies), computer literacy (which had developed in the 1980s as a response to the launch of personal computers and which described the computer as a means to achieving a specified outcome); and information literacy (finding evaluating using and sharing information) (Belshaw 2012)."

I found many ways to define it during my research: "According to my research:

"Digital literacy means having the necessary skills to live, learn, and work in a society where communication and access to information are increasingly through digital technologies such as internet platforms, social media networks, and mobile devices.

(https://www.westernsydney.edu).

The definition by the American Library Association Task Force is referenced in the Workforce Innovation and Opportunity Act." Jamie Harris Adult Education Program specialist at the Department of Labor. "Digital Literacy is defined by the International Museum and Library Services Act of 2010 as **"the ability to use information and communication technologies to find, evaluate, create and communicate information, requiring both cognitive and technical skills."**

We cannot talk about digital literacy without having in mind the tools and other components that allow us to have the ability to use technology; for instance, I would say that for us to integrate into the digital society, we need to be ready and equipped with tools such as internet and computers that allow us to be fully integrated and have full participation.

As I have always mentioned before in my pages above, we must balance our psycho and emotions; digital literacy requires both cognitive and technical skills. This is where we need to balance our emotions in addition to being able to acquire technical skills in association with cognitive skills to put learning functioning. Some researchers say that: "digital literacy is the ability to use information and communication technologies to find, evaluate, create, and communicate information, requiring both cognitive and technical skills." (https:// alair.ala.org-handle.

DIGITAL LITERACY: The four fundamental pillars

COMPREHENSION: "Ability to extract ideas, implicit or explicit, from any digital medium."

INTERDEPENDENCE: "This means that digital media or information is not created in isolation but with the aim of being disseminated on other channels."

This means that from what I experienced, there is an abundance of media that can be used or shared with one another.

SOCIAL FACTORS: "Sharing content on the internet is no longer a personal thing, but a relevant social factor. It's through this medium that we can find out everything that's going on in the world."

SELECTION: "This is related to understanding and maintaining information, making it accessible and useful for a long time. Example: cloud platforms"

FOUR COMPONENTS OF DIGITAL LITERACY

- Finding
- Evaluating
- Creating
- Communicating information

Since I am putting practice digital literacy in the classrooms now, I identified some benefits that digital Literacy brings to students' attention:

It enhances students' collaboration and engagement, creates more opportunities for collaboration, and students are able to respect others' opinions' and ideas which they are aware of self-awareness. Likewise, as I have mentioned above, it improves digital equity among students, supports lifelong skills, and increases online security, etc.

Below, I am sharing an activity named Make Me Digital that I put into practice with my students, an experience of how they will react to the AI impact in the learning process. I created this activity to get their emotional impact on technology and also to introduce them smoothly to this new Tech-Social Dimension, as I described above in my chapters. Make Me Digital Activity is to make students get in contact with traditional teaching in transition to the digital realm. Students will touch both worlds. However, they are obviously transitioning from the traditional to the digital.

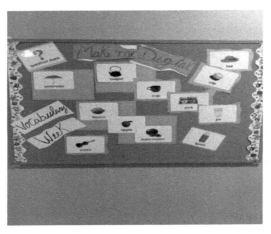

MAKE ME DIGITAL

This is an activity that I have my adult ESOL students do in order for them to get used to and comfortable with the digital world and expand their mindset by exploring vocabulary and grammar previously learned in class. Students will also use Burlington English, a language learning platform that uses AI to practice listening and record their voices for practing pronunciation as well. Different teaching skills will also be put into practice, such as: Digital skills, Cultural Awareness, and Critical Thinking.

How to puzzle Make Me Digital Activity?

- Students take pictures with their devices from the bulletin board with traditional flashcards displayed.

- Students critically think about sentences and relate previous grammar learned in class.
- Students will work with digital cards from their devices
- Students will go on google to look for vocabulary pictures and meaning.

Students Experience Comments

- "This activity made us work in teams."
- "We learned how to use different sentences from different vocabulary."
- "We used smartphones to bring the flashcards digitally to the group work."
- "Communication – collaboration- sharing different ideas" –
- "We digitalized the cards with our smartphones."

The Impact of the Activity

"It made us change our capacity of thinking because of the digital material used in a smartphone, to make different flash cards digital. The impact of not touching the flashcards as we did traditionally made us think.

The use of google to search for the same vocabulary also helped us learn more and to expand our mindset.' Luxon Cleger (ESOL student)

As I have mentioned in this book, the emotional impact is present. We have to know how to adapt and accommodate to this new dimensions' atmosphere.

GOOGLING AND ITS POWER

GOOGLE is indeed a powerful tool. Google has the answers that we are looking for. Nowadays, the world relies on GOOGLE in order to find the answers they need and use them for studies or other searches, even though Googling an answer most of the time isn't efficient. *"Simply Googling and the answer does not provide students with true, deep learning. And while most students understand how to use a search engine, it is up to teachers to provide students with the additional skills to bring the answers to the next level".*

As I continued with my research, naturally, I found several ways teachers can implant digital literacy skills into internet browsing. Students should first, in my opinion, be aware of safe and trustworthy sources. Indeed, students must know the difference between the sources that they are using.

"Students need to know the difference between trustworthy and untrustworthy sources."

- "Is their source an academic website or a marketing company?"
- "When was the source last updated?"
- "How many sites link to this source as a reference?"
- "Is the information presented in objective or biased language?"

There is no need for students to know all the pieces of software; however, it is crucial that teachers stimulate students to learn the software necessary for them to use in order to fulfill what is required. Therefore, I am still concerned about the teaching and learning process through digital literacy. In fact, it worries me when I feel and see that the four skills of learning and teaching are not put in place appropriately. Learning is happening through a virtual space, which I call the Tech-Social Dimension. This tech social dimension is separating us from using our motor skills, for example, writing skills. We need to use our hands to hold onto a pen or pencil to bring information to our brains.

I am not saying that by using digital, we cannot learn; we can learn similarly, but we also must take into consideration our emotional state during this learning process because it is new to us as human beings. As human beings, we need to see, touch, smell, feel, and taste. Here in this world of tech social dimension, as I call it, we can only touch and see sometimes. Our behavior and our psycho– emotions become threatened by technology.

Consequently, this quote affirms that: *"It is crucial for schools and district administrators to emphasize teacher digital literacy to avoid policies that simply mandate placing technology into the hands of students without thought for how that technology will be used."* At the same time, the fact that students use technology without knowing how to use it brings frustration to them, and it can also cause anxiety, which, when interrelated, can also cause stress in youth. According to DR Qiaoqing Zong, as mentioned above, *"On the other hand, Heart Broken Syndrome affects mostly the middle age and or the senior population. However, we cannot neglect the Heart Broken Syndrome impact on the young population; (young people can also suffer from heart broken syndrome because of emotional stress or another kind of stress."*

I would say that there is nothing for us to be afraid of because technology brings us updates for a better life in the future.

According to this quote: **"Teach students how to draw a strong conclusion.** Sure, students might find the right answer to a problem, but what use is that search if they've only memorized the logic to get them there? It's up to teachers to teach that logic and to contextualize the answer". In this case, teachers should use the four skills for teaching logic and go beyond contextualizing the logic whatsoever; the teacher can vary his or her method of inputting information into the learning process so that long-term memory can take place by adequately storing information. *"Long-term memory refers* *to the memory process in the brain that takes information from the short-term memory store and creates long-lasting memories. These memories can be from an hour ago or several decades ago. Long-term memory can hold an unlimited amount of information for an indefinite period."*

Oct. 13, 2021 (https://www.medicalnewstoday.com/articles/long-term memory.)

BEHAVIORAL-EMOTIONAL ADAPTATION AND ACCOMMODATION

"Digitally literate teachers see technology for all of its creative potential rather than something they are mandated to do in a step-by-step fashion. Digital literacy doesn't require that teachers become experts, but it does require that they understand the digital tools that can unlock their deeper teaching potential."

Behavioral and emotional accommodation begins to take place when teachers are looking to unbutton their potential as professionals who can create materials to teach to the point that they are being told to follow instructions and even sometimes have lesson plans already built for them from platforms. All in all, it is the teacher's emotional state playing the puzzle of teaching now and in the future.

By having the lesson plan ready for me, I think that I still need to create a way within that lesson plan already to touch it and make it as dynamic as possible according to the syllabus and the curriculum being used, of course, and to have into considerations the state standard correlations and more.

It plays with my emotions and my way of implementing a lesson plan that, for years, I have been able to maneuver its way of adapting to my students' needs and expectations.

We have to consider these two crucial factors for our recent adult immigrant arrival students: what are their needs and expectations?

Lesson plans should be implemented based on these two crucial factors that I found interesting in their learning process.

EXAMPLES OF WEBSITES FOR LANGUAGE LEARNERS AND LESSON PLANNING WITH AI:

Lesson Planning with AI by COABE; https://coabe.org/streamline-lesson-plannig-with-artificial-intelligence-a-step-by-step-guide-for-adult-educators/

Prompts for Language Learners: https://myenglishdomain.com/chatgpt-prompt-for-language-learners/

Youtube Videos- AI for Adult ESOL:

https://www.youtube.com/results?Search_query=using+AI=in+adult+esol+education+

These websites are helpful, however, we still need to pay attention to the emotional part of it. I am not saying that they are wrong, but yet we still need to be aware of AI pros and cons in terms of accuracy and errors as well. At the same time, I would say that Generative AI is helpful. Why use GAI?

It might save time – better target students' needs- it could be Creative––stimulate scenario-based conversations – It can create quizzes based on your content.

It can possibly be translated if necessary as well.

We can also use other platforms as tools to help us, such as futuretools.io

Google Gemini: https://gemini.google.com/

Again, I am stressing the awareness of using these GAIs because of their accuracy and errors that might occur sometimes. Can we trust it 100%? Well, I would say we just need to be alert and correct the errors that we as human beings can encounter as we are in contact with the AI dimension.

Chat GPT

Lesson Plan: Exploring Science

Level B2 Adult English Learners

Theme: Science

Duration: 45 minutes

Delivery Method: Remote teaching via zoom

Teaching Approach: Task-based Language Teaching

Student Interaction Format: Group work

Objective: to increase students' speaking skills through exploring scientific concepts and discussions.

Materials: - videos related to scientific topics (e.g., TED Talks, educational YouTube videos)

- Online whiteboard or shared document for collaborative note-taking
- The lesson's outline includes the following: 1- Warm-Up
- 2- Introduction to Task-
- 3- Chat Prompts- communication skills: Get the Chatbot to ask you questions/engage in role-play
- Written Assessment- ask your GAI to provide feedback on grammar, syntax, spelling, and vocabulary
- Enhance homework

- Ask your GAI to provide feedback on grammar, syntax, spelling, and vocabulary.
- Input texts written by your students, and Chat GPT will generate feedback on areas for improvement.
- Create readings or vocabulary lists for learners to memorize based on topic or class content with translation to their native languages.

CHAPTER – III

ADULT LEARNERS LIMITED TO DIGITAL LITERACY

The Seven Elements

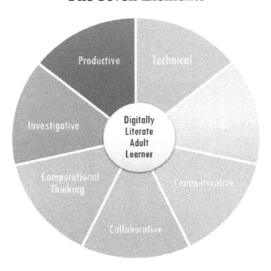

During this Pandemic, I have seen the importance of digital Literacy in the Adult Learners population that I teach. The Pandemic endorsed the importance of Adult Learners with limited digital literacy access. I had the chance to learn and grow in this area due to the circumstances that we were in at that time. During my research, I found this digital literacy Framework for Adult Learners wheel interesting because: *"The seven elements seen in the Digital Literacy Framework wheel cannot exist isolated from each other, and because digital literacy affects the life, education, and employment of adult learners, all are needed to facilitate success in each area."* https://www.learning.com- blog-reasons digital literacy.

I am going to mention four elements that I consider essential below:

TECHNICAL

"The technical element consists of foundational digital skills, which include powering on and off devices, accessing tools and applications from devices, using the mouse and touchpad, and troubleshooting. An example of this element in an adult learner's life is using the touch screen at the doctor's office to check-in."

COMMUNICATIVE

"With this element, individuals share a variety of resources with others using various platforms in employment. Writing a professional e-mail or memorandum requires professional communication. In everyday life, individuals who post images or add comments on social media use the communicative element."

INVESTIGATIVE

"Similar to information literacy, the investigative element highlights an individual's ability to search, identify, and validate the information. This is essential for adult learners to sort through the extensive amount of information provided in the digital space, especially in employment if they are required to order office supplies of quality and reasonable prices."

PRODUCTIVE

"The productive element highlights participation in the digital environment with content creation and duration of resources. This element requires an individual's motivation and application of all the elements to be successful. In the digital environment, publishing content on a blog or creating a video for social media are all part of content creation." Jamie Harris, Adult Education Program Specialist at the Maryland Department of Labor.

(https://rossieronline.usc.edu/blog/teacher-digital-
literacy/)

I also found that teachers should take into consideration the reasons why digital literacy should be taught. I am pointing only a few that should touch our emotional behavior that I encounter as crucial to be taught.

IMPROVING TECHNOLOGY

The velocity of changes must have an impact on teachers' emotional and psychological state of being. After all, teachers are working with new materials, new concepts, and new strategies for teaching. Consider the following: "Technology changes or improves as years go on, *and we can now see the velocity of its improvement.*" In the same way, teachers are called teacherpreneurs, so there is a need for teachers to know and develop the digital world to master their lessons and be able to demonstrate their capacity to input information to their students. Indeed, it is their emotion that should be put in the position of understanding, which I describe as the Tech Society Dimension. Everyone looks forward to their own dimension so that they adapt or accommodate themselves. We can create a culture where society can technologically fit without having much to suffer emotionally.

*(*https://rossieronline.usc.edu/blog/teacher-digital-
literacy/)

Technology fits in with its essential power of demonstrating its creative ways of helping students to navigate in different directions in the classroom, such as having visual learners work with illustrations on their tablets, and audio learners can record a situation or a teacher's lecture to be reviewed further on. On the **other hand,** technology can also help teachers be creative in terms of assisting learners to create projects like videos or written stories. *"Digital literacy is required in order to set the standards and boundaries for this kind of differentiation."*

(https://rossieronline.usc.edu/blog/teacher-digital-literacy/).

Students need to know and understand how to socialize in the technological dimensions. There is an urge for students to realize that online behavior is also crucial while using it. We can easily hurt one another if one does not use appropriate vocabulary or follow the social norms applied online.

"Cyberbullying is bullying that takes place using electronic technology and is a pervasive issue in schools and online communities. And while today's students may be digital natives, they still need to be taught that social norms apply to online behavior." In the words of DR Qiaoqing Zhong: "On the other hand, heart broken syndrome affects mostly the middle age and or the senior population. However, we cannot neglect the heart broken syndrome impact on the young population; (young people can also suffer from heart broken syndrome because of emotional stress or other kinds of stress." In this case, I would point out the Cyberbullying stress where students suddenly appear to have a strange attitude toward their parents or colleagues because of it. Furthermore, most of the time, the students don't reveal the cyberbullying.

The young population can be easily impacted by new technology due to the fact that they are more vulnerable to technology. For this reason, it is crucial to have control of the technology used among youngsters.

I believe that students should be educated about cyberbullying to help students who are being bullied. Young populations are so adept at using digital tools that they do not realize that photos posted on Instagram or the apps being used to record their voice or pictures could also be used for journalism projects.

CHAPTER – IV

PREVENTING OURSELVES FROM BEING EMOTIONALLY HURT. WHY?

We still need to prevent this because we are still not sure about the future of health and education. What will education look like? We do have an idea of what we are going through. Nevertheless, we are still in the process of developing AI to improve the teaching and learning input through technology, such as having new educational platforms that will allow the educational realm to be independent and have critical thinking. We are uncertain of where education is going to end. I assume that this is a concern that all educators, parents, and caregivers are having. Meanwhile, we can ask how we should balance our emotions to adapt to the new normal dimension.

The most important thing right now is to get ourselves into digital literacy so that we can master technology. That way, we can share ideas and become an active part of the technology society. We can also strive for success while trying to reach our goals in this new society and communicate better with one another. Artificial intelligence vocabulary has become part of this new standard society dimension.

Our emotions become part of this new society where we can play and trick our minds on how to adapt and accommodate to this **Tech-Social Dimension.**

Tech-Social Dimension

As I have described in my book 'Educating Through Pandemic-"Traditional Classroom Vs. Virtual Space", we need to balance ourselves emotionally, and that is why I describe between dimensions. I divided it into four stages, and I found myself comfortable and adaptable to the new normal.

Doctor Phil Bartle described the technological Dimension: "The technological dimension of culture is its capital, tools and skills, and ways of dealing with the physical environment. It is the interface between humanity and nature." March 22, '12.

Hence, I believe in the Tech-Social Dimension that I describe as another way that I found myself believing that we can create a culture where the society can technologically fit without having much to suffer emotionally.

This Tech-Social Dimension is what I call it because we are going through technological dimensions. For each dimension, we need to be able to adapt and create a culture of what is better for us in terms of our behavior as human beings. We need to take care of both our hearts and minds. It is hard to remember that we are going too fast.

I would say that we still must prevent it because we still need to take care of our emotions.

What is the technological Dimension?

"The technological dimension of culture is its capital, tools and skills, and ways of dealing with the physical environment. It is the interface between humanity and nature" March 22, '12. For this reason, I would highlight that the "technological dimension of culture" is interfering with our minds and has an impact on our attitudes and behavior. Indeed, our emotional state is being hit by this "technological culture" that is aggressively forcing us to work and to learn new things faster. I have nothing against its velocity; however, it is our way of processing information that seems to have a role here in being violated by this velocity. This could have an impact on our psycho-emotional state.

As DR. Qiaoqing Zhong expresses an example from a patient: "It's a perfect example of our brain-heart connection." Patient said, *"The emotional stress we have in our brain can lead to responses in the heart, and not much is known about this condition. Of course, everyone's threshold for stress is different. Loneliness and social isolation are significant risk factors."*

According to this quote, I can clearly see the connection between our brain and our heart. What do you think makes you feel that way?

When we connect teaching and learning with social isolation by using technology for individual learning, the risks can be obviously noticeable because we can have students starting to feel lonely and showing signs of anxiety, depression, etc. This is because they can sometimes feel frustrated in the process of adapting to the new Tech-Social Culture––the culture where the world must adapt now and more soon. Therefore, culture is learned. We should evaluate its process and see how culture is seen.

"Socialization is what happens every day of our lives, is not planned. It involves our learning our identities, the nature of reality, and how to get along with others." (Phil Bartle, Ph.D.) Certainly, if we start working or studying individually, there will be a major change in our behavior and also in our emotions. Our mind needs to think differently and to work faster in order to follow the changes.

CHAPTER – V

WAYS OF DEFINING ARTIFICIAL INTELLIGENCE

"Artificial intelligence (AI) involves using computers to do things that traditionally require human intelligence. AI can process large amounts of data in ways that humans cannot. The goal for AI is to be able to do things like recognize patterns, make decisions, and judge like humans."

(https://www.linkedin.com>pulseartificial-intelligence).

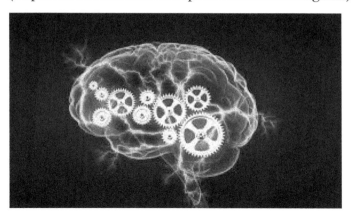

WHA IS ARTIFICIAL INTELIGENCE?

(hcltech.com)

"What is artificial intelligence (AI)? Artificial intelligence is the stimulation of human intelligence processes by machines, especially computer systems. Specific applications of AI include expert systems, natural language processing, speech recognition, and machine vision."

(tech target.com- definition-Artificial intelligence)

"Artificial intelligence (AI) is defined as machine intelligence that mimics a human mind's problem-solving and decision-making capabilities to perform various tasks. All AI types use machine learning, deep learning, and neural networks to evolve to higher levels."

Spiceworks.com/tech/artificial-intelligence/articles/narrow-general-super-ai-difference/

WHAT IS ARTIFICIAL INTELLIGENCE IN EDUCATION?

In education, we see artificial intelligence as a way of helping both students and teachers accomplish their goals and expectations in terms of inputting information because AI provides us with a diversity of technological tools capable of helping us go through the lesson plans. It can even create lesson plans according to the theme and topic being learned. In addition, it can provide us with listening activities, audio, and videos capable of demonstrating its potential in delivering academic information. For example, the Burlington English program is a good source for adult learning because of its academic feature as an Ed-Tech source of learning. I am using it to teach professionals and non-professional adult learners. I found it valuable in terms of its virtual teaching and learning process.

WHAT IS THE PURPOSE OF ARTIFICIAL INTELLIGENCE?

"In summary, the goal of AI is to provide software that can reason on input and explain on output. AI will provide human-like interactions with software and offer decision support for specific tasks, but it's not a replacement for humans- and won't be anytime soon." (SA. com, an _insights analytics)

"The theory of the development of computer systems that are able to perform tasks normally requiring human intelligence, such as vision perception, speech recognition, decision-making and translation between languages."

(intellipaat.com/pros-and-cons-of-ai).

TYPES OF ARTIFICIAL INTELLIGENCE

Narrow AI – "Dedicated to assisting with or taking over specific tasks." Narrow AI is designed to perform tasks that normally require human intelligence, but it operates under a limited set of constraints and is task-specific. It doesn't possess understanding or consciousness, but rather, it follows pre-programmed rules or learns patterns from data."

"Narrow AI, also known as weak AI, refers to AI that is designed to perform a specific task or a limited range of tasks. It is the most common type of AI and is widely used in various applications such as facial recognition, speech recognition, image recognition, natural language processing, and recommendation systems."

https://www.linkedin.com/pulse/narrow-ai-vs-general-super-ahmed-banafa18/03/2023

General AI- "Takes knowledge from one domain, transfers to another domain."

Super AI: "Machines that are extremely smart compared to humans." intellipaat.com/pros-and-cons-of-ai).

"Super AI will simulate human reasoning and experiences to develop an emotional understanding, beliefs, and desires of its own. Data Processing. Narrow AI classifies data by using machine learning, natural language processing, artificial neural networks, and deep learning. "25/03/2022.

"Artificial superintelligence (ASI) is a form of AI that is capable of surpassing human intelligence by manifesting cognitive skills and developing thinking skills of its own.

Also known as super AI, artificial superintelligence is considered the most advanced, powerful, and intelligent type of AI that transcends the intelligence of some of the brightest minds, such as Albert Einstein." https://www.spiceworks.com/tech/artificial-intelligence/articles/super-artificial- intelligence/

CHAPTER – VI

FACIAL RECOGNITION

WHAT IS THE ROLE OF AI IN COMPARISON TO OUR HUMAN BRAIN?

We know that AI can not yet have feelings or emotions; however, studies show that AI can recognize facial expressions and emotions.

WHAT IS FACIAL EMOTION RECOGNITION?

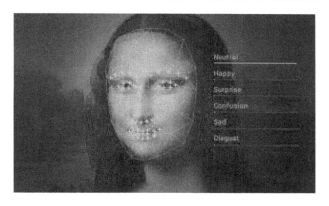

"Facial Emotion Recognition (FER) is the technology that analyses facial expressions from both static images and videos in order to reveal information on one's emotional state."

"They can listen to voice inflections and start to recognize when those inflections correlate with stress or anger. Machines can analyze images and pick up subtleties in micro-expressions on humans' faces that might happen even too fast for a person to recognize."

08/03/2019https://mitsloan.mit.edu/ideas-made-to-matter/emotion-ai-

AI systems are trained to analyze facial expressions, vocal intonations, and even text to infer human emotions. Through machine learning algorithms, AI can identify patterns and cues that are imperceptible to the human eye, leading to a more accurate understanding of emotions. 31/08/2023

AI in Emotion Detection: How It Works

Facial Expression Analysis

AI employs facial recognition technology to detect micro-expressions and subtle changes in facial features. This enables AI to identify emotions such as happiness, sadness, anger, and surprise. By analyzing the arrangement of facial muscles and comparing them to a vast database, AI can accurately gauge a person's emotional state.

(Hani Jbaily) Manager-client Acquisition at Data Tech Labs August 2023

Speech and Voice Analysis

The way we speak and the tone of our voice conveys a wealth of emotional information. AI algorithms can analyze voice patterns, pitch, and intonation to determine emotions like excitement, frustration, or even deceit. This technology finds applications in call centres where AI can assess customer emotions and help in providing better service.

Text and Sentiment Analysis

In the digital age, emotions are often expressed through text. AI algorithms can analyze written language to identify sentiment, whether it's in social media posts, reviews, or customer feedback. This information is invaluable to businesses aiming to understand public opinion about their products or services. (Hani Jbaily) Manager - Client Acquisition at Data Tech Labs August 2023

Despite all of these AI facial recognition tasks, there is still a barrier to be covered in terms of facial recognition with masks. Researchers found out that during the pandemic, people wearing masks posed challenges to facial recognition. However, researchers said that: "companies are working to overcome this, focusing their technology on the facial features visible above these masks."

Equity and AI

Researchers say that:

- Facial recognition with older adults becomes less accurate when people age
- In terms of racial and gender bias, studies have shown that facial recognition is less effective in identifying people of color and women.

Marketers and advertisers in campaigns

Marketers often consider gender, age, and ethnicity when targeting groups for a product or idea. Marketers can use facial recognition to define those audiences at stores or events.

Risks: your facial data can be collected and stored, often without your permission. Hackers could access and steal that data.

In addition to the above research, I would like to add more information as I continuously look for AI knowledge.

I believe that we all should know that facial recognition is already being used in our society. At starts with the phones that we use. When we go for our grocery shopping as well, the security cameras catch us as we go by them.

Here are some other places that we can also find facial recognition:

In cellphones: Apple first used facial recognition to unblock its iPhone X and access your digital wallet. The company has continued using facial recognition in new models. Apple says the chance of a random face unblocking your phone is about one in 1 million. Likewise, facial recognition software is being used nationwide on campus to improve security and to manage who is on campus.

We use Social media every day and many times a day. "Facebook uses an algorithm to spot faces when one uploads a photo to its platform. The Social media company asks if you want to tag people in your photos. If you say yes, it creates a link to their profiles; Facebook can recognize faces with 98 percent accuracy."

This is what I found out about how Facial recognition works:

"Facial recognition uses technology and biometrics – typically through AI – to identify human faces. It maps features from a photograph or video and then compares the information with a database of known faces to find a match. facial recognition can help verify a person's identity but also raises privacy issues." This is how it works:

1. "Software is presented with at least one video or image that shows an individual's face."
2. "Software scans videos and images to create a map of a person's facial features called a facial signature. This includes data like their eye's precise location, scars, or other facial differences.
3. "Facial recognition systems compare the individual's facial signature to its database. Today, many databases contain tens of millions to billions of images."
4. "The facial recognition system determines whether or not the facial signature is a match to anything in its database. Some systems may also calculate an accuracy score or provide alternatives."

A TRIP TO MIT

We can scan and read from the floor, as I mentioned in one of my chapters above.

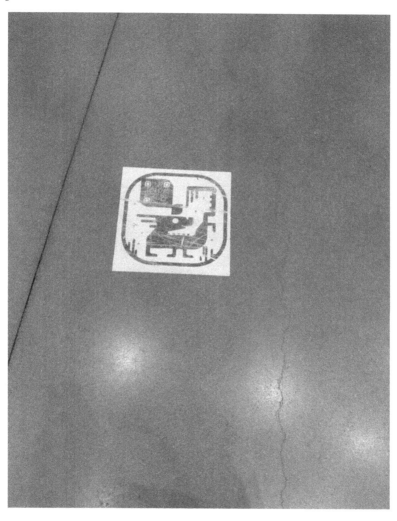

Flow (2018)
Interactive Visual Effects By Karl Sims
BS 1984, MS 1987

Move in front of the display to interact with this exhibit, but please do not touch the screens or the camera.

This augmented-reality exhibit allows you to interact with various computer simulations including fluid flow, particle systems, and other image-processing and graphics effects. The exhibit cycles through 10 different effect modes, each lasting about one minute. The cycle of effects varies from day to day, so your experience may differ depending on when you visit.

An infrared depth camera above the display senses your distance and motions which influence the simulations. Custom software for this project was written in C, OpenCL, and OpenGL, which runs on a workstation with an NVIDIA TITAN Xp graphics card.

This exhibit was commissioned by MIT CSAIL.
For more info: http://www.karlsims.com/flow.html
#SimsAtCSAIL

Privacy note: the camera images are used for interaction purposes only and are not being recorded.

Interactive Visual Effects By: Karl Sims

Pictures of myself as I interact with the camera, different motions, and different pictures in front of the camera.

"It senses my distance and motions, which influence the simulations."

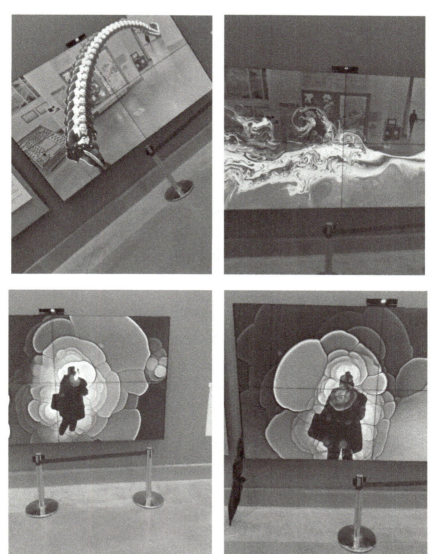

HUMAN-LIKE CAPABILITIES OF SUPER AI

SUPER AI – CONSCIOUSNESS-BELIEFS-DESIRES-COGNITION-EMOTIONAL INTELLIGENCE-SUBJECTIVE EXPERIENCES-BEHAVIORAL INTELLIGENCE-

We need to understand that AI can't feel. Even though *"Apart from replicating multi-faceted human behaviour,* whatever that AI does or may do in the future is based on the capacity of human beings who want to let it be. To be or not to be? That will be the question. *"ASI develops emotional understanding, beliefs, and desires of its own, based on the comprehension capability of the AI."* Meanwhile, we will watch the show and also play on it. Accommodation and adaptation are the two principal factors I would say in order for us to know how to emotionally balance the impact of the future AI changing our behavior and way of thinking as well.

HUMAN-LIKE CAPABILITIES OF SUPER AI

"Machines with super intelligence are self-aware and can think of abstractions and interpretations that humans cannot. This is because the human brain's thinking ability is limited to a set of a few billion neurons. Apart from replicating multi-faceted human behavioral intelligence, ASI can also understand and interpret human emotions and experiences. ASI develops emotional understanding, beliefs, and desires of its own, based on the comprehension capability of the AI."

"ASI finds application in virtually all domains of human interests, be it math, science, arts, sports, medicine, marketing, or even emotional relations. An ASI system can perform all the tasks humans can, from defining a new mathematical theorem for a problem to exploring physics law while venturing into outer space.

ASI systems can quickly understand, analyze, and process circumstances to stimulate actions."

As a result, the decision-making and problem-solving capabilities of super-intelligent machines are expected to be more precise than humans."

"Currently, superintelligence is a theoretical possibility rather than a practical reality as most of the development today in computer science and AI is inclined toward <u>artificial narrow intelligence (ANI)</u>. This implies that AI programs are designed to solve only specific problems."

"Machine learning and deep learning algorithms are further advancing such programs by utilizing neural networks as the algorithms learn from the results to iterate and improve upon themselves."

"Thus, such algorithms process data more effectively than previous AI versions. However, despite the advancements in neural nets, these models can only solve problems at hand, unlike human intelligence."

As I analyzed all these quotes above about ASI (Artificial Super Intelligence), I became more curious about how human beings are going to react to ASI if "the decision-making and problem-solving capabilities of super-intelligent machines are expected to be more precise than humans." There will be a need to establish the emotional status in addition to balancing the impact of its powerful performance on human beings. The impact could be feasible if everyone is digitally educated.

CHAPTER – VII

ARTIFICIAL INTELLIGENCE: ITS BENEFITS AND PROS

We all know that artificial intelligence can help students grow in most areas of education. Nowadays, we have many platforms (programs) that can help students provide adequate and accurate information and even needs and expectations about the content that they are looking for to learn. In adult education, for instance, we have the Burlington English platform, where students (adults) can find multiple ways to learn English. In fact, the Burlington English platform, a program for adults, offers comprehensive General English Courses as well as a wide range of career courses. It provides a complete language-learning solution. It was built from the ground up using the best methodologies identified by linguistics, educators, and software developers for overcoming the specific challenges of language learning. It is convenient because learners can go to the burlingtonenglish.com website and download the corresponding app for mobile devices. It offers an unparalleled Pronunciation Course to help users perfect their pronunciation, listening, and speaking skills.

Furthermore, from my experience, while teaching with Burlington English, I have seen progress with my adult students.

Burlington English, as mentioned above, offers a unique speech trainer to help users perfect their pronunciation and listening skills. That said, there are all four language learning skills: listening, speaking, reading, and writing, as well as grammar and life skills lessons, which I have applied with my students and have benefited from their progress. Burlington English allows students to watch videos with respect to the content of the lesson with constant repetition, using activities for students to listen and repeat in sequence to the lesson being learned. My job is to manage the program according to the school curriculum and observe my students' progress during the class period.

I have noticed that students also seem to be motivated to learn since they are not only reading and listening but also practicing. In addition, they are also listening to audio, watching videos, playing listening, and repeating vocabulary games in the context of the modules.

From the teacher's perspective, I always encourage my students to practice the vocal recording of the vocabulary. This helps them memorize the lesson word lists more rapidly and adds to the analysis of their pronunciation.

Teachers can follow students' progress in terms of their highest scores, completion percentages, and overall time spent working on the platform and assign work as needed. Over time, students receive individualized feedback on their pronunciation when they record their voices in various activities.

There are many programs out there to help students and teachers achieve their goals. Burlington English is a language learning platform that uses AI effectively; however, teachers and students still need to be technologically proficient. As I have delineated above, digital literacy has become a crucial skill for any human being now and in the future.

PROS OF ARTIFICIAL INTELLIGENCE

Artificial intelligence can save humans time for productive tasks. Human beings often make mistakes when performing or doing any specific task. I would say that this may vary from the individual's intelligence perspective. We have to admit that artificial intelligence accomplishes a specific task without an error most of the time. Again, this may depend on how well such a program is designed and programmed.

Below, I identify the following from my research:

"Unlike humans, machines do not require breaks to recover from tiredness and boost productivity. There are many day-to-day tasks accomplished by a human that are repetitive. The efficiency of a human reduces while continuously performing the same job. Moreover, it is a fact that a human worker can be productive only for 8–10 hours per day."

Otherwise, AI machines can perform tasks for a long period without having to stop or take a break. It works continuously with no break in between. In addition, no complaining about getting tired. At the same time, human beings cannot be compared to an AI in terms of jobs or task performance yet in making the right decisions. For example:

"One of the advantages of Artificial Intelligence is its ability to make the right decision. There are no emotions attached to the AI-based machines that help prevent hampering efficiency. The machines that are built using Artificial Intelligence are capable of making logical decisions as well. A human would examine a situation by considering many factors. These factors may influence the decision emotionally or practically. However, the machines give accurate results as they are programmed to make logical decisions. AI-powered machines use cognitive computing that helps them make practical decisions in real-time."

I have considered this quote: "...These factors may influence the decision emotionally or practically. However, the machines give accurate results as they are programmed to make logical decisions. AI cognitive computing that helps them make practical decisions in real-time." As human beings, we are surrounded by emotions. This can make us make mistakes at any time. This is why I consider this quote because it is crucial to know, and we should not discuss it in comparison to humans against AI. AI, obviously, does not have emotions yet. I say yet because they may be built with emotions in the future; nonetheless, they will probably be different from humans.

Back to my thought, I defend that AI is efficient in terms of considering its cognitive computing power in task productivity in relation to differences to humans. Additionally, another benefit of AI is all the digital assistance that we can find in both the healthcare and education fields.

a) "Another advantage of AI is that AI-powered applications also provide digital assistance. Today, most organizations make use of digital assistants to perform automated tasks. This helps save human resources. Some digital assistants can program to make a website for us. The use of digital assistants has revolutionized the healthcare industry as well. Now, doctors can look after their patients from remote locations with the help of digital assistants that provide real-time data on patients."

b)-"Digital assistants also help us in our day-to-day activities. There are many practical applications of AI-based digital assistants, such as Google Maps, Grammarly, Alexa, and many more. Google Maps helps us travel from one place to another, while Alexa executes voice searches to give us results. Another interesting digital assistant is Grammarly, which helps correct grammar. It auto-corrects the text to improve our writing skills. These applications make AI advantageous over other technologies. Further, in this blog on the pros and cons of AI, we will discuss the cons of AI."

"One of the reasons AI is known to make unbiased decisions is because it has no emotions. AI, along with other technologies, can make decisions faster than

human beings and carry out actions rapidly. While making decisions, we need to analyze a lot of factors, which may take time, but AI can review all the relevant aspects much faster than a human. This helps businesses develop an edge over their competitors as AI provides them with enough time to make better decisions."

"It is no brainer that AI is powering several inventions across the globe that will help humans solve complex problems. For example, doctors recently leveraged the prowess of AI-based technologies to predict breast cancer during earlier stages."

'On a far grander scale, AI is poised to have a major effect on sustainability, climate change and environmental issues. Ideally and partly through the use of sophisticated sensors, cities will become less congested, less polluted, and generally more livable.'

WHAT ARE CONS OF AI?

According to researchers, they are trying to replace human doctors with AI doctors. Obviously, AI cannot take over the human doctor's feelings or thoughts. As a matter of fact, we know that AI is not capable yet of having emotions.

There are various pros and cons when we talk about artificial intelligence here. I will be talking about both the pros and cons of it according to my research. Below, I chose this picture of the cons of artificial intelligence:

1. High Costs of Creation

"The creation of machines empowered with Artificial Intelligence is very costly. For a large-scale project, the price might reach up to millions of dollars. Thus, for a small-scale business, it is not possible to implement AI. For companies with large revenues too, the cost of the development of an AI project may be felt high due to the features, functionalities, or scope with which it is designed."

"The cost of development also depends on the hardware and software the companies use. Moreover, to meet the demands of a highly changing world, the hardware and software should be regularly updated. AI-powered devices are built employing complex codes, algorithms, software, and hardware. The maintenance of these components requires great effort and costs very high. However, in the future, the cost of developing machines using AI may reduce due to the invention of advanced tools that will help create them easily."

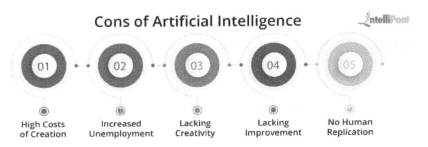

2. *Increased Unemployment*

In the not-so-distant future, the rapid advancement of artificial intelligence will bring about unprecedented levels of automation, leading to a profound impact on the global workforce. While AI has undoubtedly revolutionized various industries, there is an unmistakable human toll associated with its progress.

As machines become increasingly capable of performing complex tasks, many traditional jobs once held by hardworking individuals are now being taken over by algorithms and robots. The consequences are all too real, as individuals who once found dignity and purpose in their work are now faced with the harsh reality of unemployment. The loss of jobs not only affects livelihoods but also undermines the human connection and sense of community that is fostered through meaningful employment.

3. Lacking Creativity

"Machines cannot become as creative as humans. Artificial Intelligence can provide functionalities to learn from data but cannot make the machines mimic the exact human brain and skills. The accuracy of the results from an AI-powered machine depends on the level of analytics used by the creator." As a matter of fact, Artificial Intelligence cannot recreate anything or think. It is controlled by human beings, or, in other words, its program is under human being supervision.

"Although AI can collaborate with other technologies such as IoT, Big Data, advanced sensors, and many more to give the best automation, the smartness and creativity of AI-based machines depend on how intelligent and creative the algorithms are created by humans. Therefore, AI is bound to rules and algorithms and cannot become as creative as humans."

"Russel also pointed out that AI is not currently equipped to understand language fully. This shows a distinct difference between humans and AI now: Humans can translate machine language and understand it, but AI can't do the same for human language. However, if we reach a point where AI is able to understand our languages, AI systems would be able to read and understand everything ever written."

"Humans have created machines to save time and effort from doing non-essential repetitive tasks. AI-powered machines work on algorithms, mathematical computing, and cognitive technologies." While AI can achieve impressive levels of complexity, it cannot currently truly reason and act autonomously like a human. Machines are often deemed intelligent due to their capabilities, but they cannot make independent judgments based on ethical or moral considerations. They rely solely on their programming, and encountering unforeseen circumstances might lead to malfunctions or unpredictable outcomes. Therefore, implementing AI in situations requiring significant judgment and ethical decision-making could be risky and lead to failure.

CHAPTER – VIII

HUMAN BEINGS AND THE EMOTIONAL STATUS TOWARD ARTIFICIAL INTELLIGENCE

Studies show that: "An overreliance on AI technology could result in the loss of human influence- and lack in human functioning- In some parts of society. Using AI in health care could result in reduced human reasoning. For instance, applying generative AI to creative endeavors could diminish human creativity and emotional expression. Interacting with AI too much could even cause reduced peer communication and social skills. Mike Thomas"https://builtin.com/artificial-intelligence/risks-of-artificial-intelligence

With this in mind, I would say that our emotions will be alert, and our behavior toward society will also be an issue. Certainly, we have to insert a new culture in terms of accepting this new adaptation. This is where again, I can apply the Tech-Social Dimension.

We all know that human beings function through emotions. We can not do anything in life without having emotions. It seems that we are controlled by them, in my point of view. Researchers think that: *"As AI becomes smarter and more dexterous, the same tasks will require fewer humans. And while AI is estimated to create 97 million new jobs by 2025, many employees won't have the skills needed for these technical roles and could get left behind if companies don't upskill their workforces".*

As a matter of fact, most of us are afraid that "Technology is going to replace us." For this reason, we seemed to be all astonished by its velocity by watching the AI's work and following it. We think about where it is taking us. At the same time, technology is here to help us have a better understanding of the world and have the world close to us. That said, I would say that technology is making us think faster, better, and be proactive in our daily lives. For example, when we use technology for communication, for news, for health and education, etc.

AI is now implemented in society, and its dimension is huge. Certainly, the population needs to be digitally literate in order to understand this Tech Social Dimension that I describe above in Chapter IV. The tech-social Dimension is another way that I found myself believing that we can create a culture where the society can technologically fit without having much to suffer emotionally from its impact.

Heart Broken Syndrome may take place in the Tech-social Dimension if the population is not digitally literate in the future, I think. There is no question that anxiety, stress, and its impact will be the issue that almost everybody suffers.

What is broken heart syndrome?

"Broken heart syndrome is a temporary heart condition with symptoms like those of a heart attack. You may think you're having a heart attack because both conditions cause shortness of breath and chest pain..." Indeed, anxiety, stress, and emotional impact of the new Tech-Social dimension, as I call it, could be factors for a cause of the Broken Heart Syndrome. Researchers highlights that: "unlike a heart attack, broken heart syndrome happens when a sudden physical or emotional stressor makes your heart muscle weaken rapidly."

In the future, McKinsey announces - "AI-powered job automation is a concern as technology is adopted in industries like marketing, manufacturing, and healthcare. By 2030, tasks that account for up to 30 percent of hours being worked in the US economy could be automated. Goldman Sachs even states that 300 million full-time jobs could be lost to AI automation." We can face serious emotional impacts in terms of job losses due to the fact that AI will be potentially ready by its power and ready to take over. The point is for us to be emotionally ready to accept and accommodate this Tech-Social Dimension. It seems that we have to learn how to adapt to this new culture being implemented in the society. We need to be prepared so that we can follow AI and understand where it is taking us. We have to be always ready to adapt to new changes. For example, in this quote below where Ford stipulates the following: "If you're flipping burgers at Mc Donald's and more automation comes in, is one of these new jobs going to be a good match for you? "or is it likely that the new jobs require lots of education or training or maybe even intrinsic talents -really strong interpersonal skills or creativity- that you might not have? Because those are the things that, at least so far, computers are not yet good at."

CHAPTER – IX

HEART BROKEN SYNDROME-
TAKOTSUBO CARDIOMYOPATHY

HEART BROKEN SYNDROME BY DR. Qiaoqing Zhong

Qiaoqing Zhong, a visiting scientist at Harvard Medical School and Beth Israel Deaconess Medical Center, is a recognized doctor in cardiovascular disease. She is also a longtime member of the ACC and AHA, whose work spans the fields of basic science and clinical medicine.

She received her MD and PhD from Central South University, China, in 2007. She also pursued clinical training in internal medicine at Xiangya Hospital and was a clinical fellow at Xiangya Second Hospital and the Center City Hospital of Changsha City. While running a cardiovascular research institution as a director in the First People's Hospital of Chenchou City, she was promoted to associate professor in 2007 and was named to an endowed chair at the Department of

Cardiovascular Medicine in the People's Hospital of Chenzhou City in 2008. From 2015-2022, she worked in Xiangya Hospital as a general cardiologist and a clinical investigator with expertise in cardiovascular disease and clinical trials.

"Doctor, I'm scared – what is happening to me? When I get upset, I develop chest pain." Broken heart syndrome or heart broken syndrome, we also call it Takotsubo cardiomyopathy. Emotional triggers occur more frequently. Takotsubo cardiomyopathy is also known as stress-induced cardiomyopathy or broken heart syndrome. It is a syndrome characterized by transient left ventricular (LV) dysfunction and a variety of wall-motion abnormalities. The most common presenting symptom is chest pain, followed by shortness of breath. Abnormal laboratory findings include elevated troponin and brain natriuretic peptide. The ECG (electrocardiograph) can show various abnormalities, including ST elevation, T-wave inversions, nonspecific ST-T (S waves and T waves – T waves segment) abnormalities, and QTc (the interval section on an electrocardiogram (EKG) reports that represents the time that your heart muscle takes to contract and then recover)prolongation.

Regional wall motion abnormality is usually seen on cardiac imaging. Compared with the general population, elderly postmenopausal women are most affected by Takotsubo cardiomyopathy. Excess catecholamine or sympathetic stimulation plays a central role in the path physiology of this cardiomyopathy.

The most common presenting symptom is chest pain, followed by shortness of breath. Takotsubo cardiomyopathy, also called broken heart syndrome, was found in two states after major natural disasters, suggesting the stress of disasters as a likely trigger, according to research to be presented at the American College of Cardiology's 63rd Annual Scientific Session. The authors call for greater awareness among emergency department physicians and other first responders.

Takotsubo cardiomyopathy, or broken heart syndrome, is a disorder characterized by a temporary enlargement and weakening of the heart muscle, which is often triggered by extreme physical or emotional stress – for example, being in a car accident or losing a child or spouse. Previous international studies have also linked broken heart syndrome to natural disasters, including the 2004 earthquake in Japan. This is the first U.S. study to examine the geographic distribution of the condition in relation to such catastrophes.

Patients with broken heart syndrome often complain of chest pain and shortness of breath, symptoms that mimic those of a heart attack, which can delay diagnosis. In addition, biomarkers in the blood and changes on electrocardiograms can raise suspicions of a possible heart attack. While broken heart syndrome typically resolves within a month or two, in the acute scenario, it can result in serious complications such as heart failure, life-threatening arrhythmias, and stroke. Previous studies by the same group found that as many as one in four patients with broken heart syndrome have some form of arrhythmia, and 1 to 7 percent suffer cardiac arrest. Many patients are diagnosed in the "Cath lab" (a cardiac catheterization lab), a specialized area in the hospital where doctors perform minimally invasive tests and advanced cardiac procedures to diagnose and treat cardiovascular disease.

When doctors see there are no blockages in the artery, or imaging reveals changes in the shape of the heart that are characteristic of broken heart syndrome.

"By and large, it is a very reversible form of cardiomyopathy, but in the acute phase, these patients need to be monitored closely to be sure they are stable and to prevent and manage problems," Pant said, adding that the impetus for the study was the increasing number of cases and a desire to find out what might trigger clusters of broken heart syndrome. "It's also something that emergency doctors and medical personnel need to be aware of as they are often on the frontlines seeing patients after disaster strikes."

Episodes are thought to be driven by the sympathetic response and surges of adrenaline in the body, similar to the well-known fight-or-flight reaction. This leads to depressed function of the apex and middle segment of the heart and increased contractility of the base, producing a balloon-like appearance.

"It's a perfect example of our brain-heart connection," Pant said, *The emotional stress we have in our brain can lead to responses in the heart, and not much is known about this condition.* Of course, everyone's threshold for stress is different. Loneliness and social isolation are significant risk factors.

"Please see the full paper: Clusters of 'Broken Hearts' May be Linked to Massive Natural Disasters: Analysis of U.S. Takotsubo

Cardiomyopathy Cases Shows Pattern to Cue Emergency Responders."
Mar 27, 2014

Below are ten points of Takotsubo Syndrome (Heart Broken Syndrome) Takotsubo Syndrome Mar 30, 2020,| Sherrie R. Webb, PA-C

Authors: Boyd B, Solh T. citation: Takotsubo cardiomyopathy: Review of broken heart syndrome. JAAPA 2020; 33:24-9.

The following are key points to remember about this review of Takotsubo cardiomyopathy:

1-Takotsubo cardiomyopathy––also called stress cardiomyopathy, apical ballooning syndrome, or broken heart syndrome––is a condition in which left ventricular (LV) dilatation and acute systolic heart failure occur, typically following an emotional or physical stressor. Ballooning of the LV occurs, most commonly in the apex (75-80%) or mid ventricle (10-20%).

2-Path physiology is uncertain; evidence suggests a surge in stress-related hormones contributes to apical ballooning via disruptions in the microvasculature or by myocardial toxicity.

3- Worldwide, 90% of cases occur in post-menopausal women. In Japan, it is more common in men. Men are more likely to develop the syndrome following physical stress.

4- The most common symptoms are chest pain, dyspnea, and dizziness. Weakness and syncope may occur. Physical findings can include lung rales, S3 gallop, jugular venous distention, tachycardia, hypotension, narrow pulse pressure, and systolic ejection murmur. Most patients have electrocardiographic changes such as ST-segment elevation or T-wave inversion. Cardiac biomarkers––troponin, creatine kinase-myocardial band, and B-type natriuretic peptide——are typically elevated.

5- The diagnosis is often made when a patient with suspected acute myocardial infarction is found at cardiac catheterization to have no coronary blockage. Revised Mayo Clinic diagnostic criteria include the following:

- Transient dyskinesis of the LV midsegments
- Regional wall motion abnormalities beyond a single pericardial vascular distribution
- Absence of obstructive coronary artery disease or acute plaque rupture
- New electrocardiographic abnormalities or modest trooping elevation
- Absence of pheochromocytoma and myocarditis

6 -Treatment requires inpatient care with cardiology services and is mainly supportive until LV function spontaneously returns, usually within 21 days of onset.

7- In stable patients, diuretics and vasodilators can be used for pulmonary congestion. Angiotensin-converting enzyme inhibitors, angiotensin II receptor blockers, and/or beta-blockers are used to reduce workload and control hypertension. Aldosterone receptor antagonists or angiotensin receptor-neprilysin inhibitors may be beneficial.

8 -For patients with unstable hemodynamics, obtain an echocardiogram to determine the presence of LV outflow tract obstruction (LVOTO).

If LVOTO is present, inotropes should not be used because they may worsen obstruction. Beta-blockers and intravenous fluids are appropriate. Vasopressors can be used. Extracorporeal membrane oxygenation can be considered in severe cases.

If LVOTO is not present, use inotropes and vasopressors or LV assist devices if needed.

9- A major goal is reducing the risk of major cerebral or vascular events, currently 7.1% within 30 days of hospitalization. Anticoagulation should be initiated in patients with large areas of cardiac hypokinesis.

10 -Atrial fibrillation is an independent risk factor for mortality. Within several weeks, 95% of patients recover whole cardiac fun.

Broken Heart Syndrome
Takotsubo cardiomyopathy

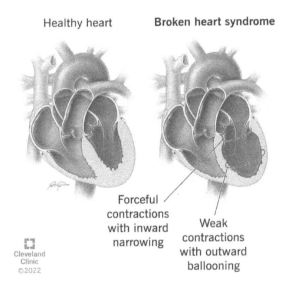

Healthy heart   Broken heart syndrome

Forceful contractions with inward narrowing

Weak contractions with outward ballooning

Cleveland Clinic ©2022

HEART BROKEN SYNDROME SYMPTOMS

SIGNS OF SYMPTOMS OF HEART BROKEN SYNDROME INCLUDE:

- Sudden, severe chest pain (angina) – a main symptom.
- Shortness of breath – a main symptom.

- Weakening of the left ventricle of your heart – a main sign
- Irregular heartbeats (arrhythmias)
- Low blood pressure (hypotension)
- Heart palpitations
- Fainting (syncope)

CHAPTER – X

ACCEPTING THE ARTIFICIAL INTELLIGENCE THE FUTURE

In my point of view, AI seems to be one of the sources that can help us Human Beings be successful in the future.

Why? I am imagining the future with technology needed for our daily life lives. As a matter of fact, we must fully work on our emotions and feelings so that we can know how to manage both our feelings and our emotions. First, we need to know how to balance our emotions because they are responsible for our feelings and, therefore, our feelings are responsible for our psycho behavior. I believe that we can also modify our attitude once the impact of AI hits our feelings and our psycho-emotions.

Are Humans asking if AI will take over? I hear people talking on the bus, and I hear people worrying about losing their jobs. As a matter of fact, some people that I interact with tell me that they are afraid of accepting AIs since they must learn how to manage them. As I was critically thinking about the future of AI in relation to human beings, I concluded that it is humans who will probably replace AI with humans without enough knowledge of how to manage AI.

AI should be accepted because of its capabilities to do multiple tasks and repetitive tasks, things that can physically hurt human beings, such as manual labor with repetitive tasks. In fact, as a result of my research for repetitive tasks on a link medium.com/@raxsuite (why manual labor on repetitive tasks is dangerous to your company), I found out that: "Employees in routinary work often stressed about how monotonous and boring their work is. Their productivity is not maximized to its potential. In fact, a study shows that 90% of employees are burdened with boring and repetitive tasks that can be automated instead.

The lack of diversity in what they do causes them to be disengaged, affecting their morale as an employee."

CHAPTER – XI

HEART DISEASE AND MENTAL HEALTH – PERSONAL DISORDERS- CULTURE IN THE DIGITAL REALM- YOUR OWN SPACE.

Creating your own space for learning will be a habit and it will create independence in the educational teaching and learning process. Our minds must be ready for the comprehensive and massive way of storing and recycling information through this new digital way. We are going through dimensions yet unknown that bring us to accelerate our thoughts and be able to change our behavior and attitude. There is no question that technology and AI are going to help us human beings to understand and guide this world better in the future however, we have to also be alert in terms of making ourselves comfortable, accommodated, and educated for the future. We must balance our emotional psycho–state so that we can fit the **Tech-Social Dimension,** as I call it.

Our heart and our mind must function in relation to the human capacity to receive and input information. We must be capable of absorbing the maximum amount of information that the AI wants us to perform and be able to retain information by AI. Besides, we must be conscious to alert ourselves about what velocity we are able to hold on to and how we are going to digest the information being input by the AI. Likewise, our Emotional state must be balanced and stable in a comfortable environment for us Human Beings to be able to process teaching, learning, and more. On page 60 of my previous book, Educating Through Pandemic Traditional Classroom Vs Virtual Space – The Education realm, I talk about the psychological versus Emotional Impact on a Virtual Classroom Environment. I created for myself a psycho-emotional dimension space balance for me to teach remotely, which I call Between Dimension. What is Between Dimension? It is to "Balance" yourself mentally, to find yourself a comfortable space, to bring yourself to know you, and finally apply your knowledge. During this period of the pandemic, we needed to understand what was going wrong with the world and try to accommodate ourselves emotionally, psychologically, and socially to survive. During the pandemic period when we could not go out to teach in person, in like manner, I found myself in need of creating the Tech-Social Dimension Culture in order to fit myself into this new AI "future world."

Adaptation + Accommodation = Balance

Adaptation

AI is causing society to transition faster in terms of technology, from physical to digital. We all know that we have to learn new ways of communication and also new ways of behaving again. We need to learn how to adapt smoothly without causing any stress or emotional distress that can affect our minds and hearts.

Accommodation

How are we going to accommodate?

It is through digital literacy education. We need to educate ourselves digitally to avoid any distress or stress so that we can mentally accept the changes and challenges of the AI.

CHAPTER – XII

SOCIAL-EMOTIONAL – EDUCATION HAS A STRONG IMPACT ON HEART DISEASE RISK

Social Emotional has a significant impact in terms of learning nowadays. This is because of the rapid way the teaching and learning process is going. The amount of want to be on the same page with education digital transformation and the desire to put into practice what one knows becomes stressful to the point that it brings education to have a strong impact on heart disease risk––the emotion of learning, the emotion of knowing new things, etc. Our mind begins to trigger the enigma of how to accommodate the rapid way of changing the traditional way of life to the near future adaptation of the new technology society realm.

This is the digital industrial revolution. As a matter of fact, a technological revolution is a period in which technologies are replaced by a new era of technology in a short period. It is a technological time of rapid progress characterized by innovations, applications, and diffusion that might cause an abrupt change in society.

"Some examples of technological revolutions were the Industrial Revolution in the 19th century."

- "The scientific-technical revolution, about 1950-1960, the Neolithic Revolution, and the Digital Revolution."
- "Western culture: financial-agricultural revolution (1600-1740)."
- "Technical Revolution or second Industrial Revolution (1870-1920)."

- "Scientific-technical revolution (1940-1970) information and telecommunications revolution, also known as Digital Revolution or Third Industrial Revolution (1975-2021)."

The fourth Industrial Revolution, the intelligence Revolution

- "Some say we're on the brink of a Fourth /industrial Revolution, aka "The intelligence Revolution" (2022).

In like manner, technology is already changing society in all parameters of our lives. The future will prove the challenge and the changes in our lifestyle. This fourth Revolution came to teach and measure our capacity to see things and teach us how to make the necessary changes in terms of social and personal behavior. Thus, in this book, I am expressing the importance of how important it is for us human beings to balance our emotions along with DR Qiaoqing Zhong's input on Heart Broken Syndrome also highlights the importance of emotional balance. She highlights how our hearts and minds function in terms of emotions. **The emotional stress we have in our brain can lead to responses in the heart, and not much is known about this condition**. Of course, everyone's threshold for stress is different. Loneliness and social isolation are significant risk factors.

"AI has come a long way since 1951 when the **first documented success of an AI computer program** was written by Christopher Strachey, whose checkers program completed a whole game on the Ferranti Mark I computer at the University of Manchester."

Although it may seem to be with us for a long time now, it is time for AI to prove its capacity and challenge human beings as human beings themselves produce them.

Researchers delineate the following: "Individualized Instruction will increase."

I still claim that we need to be prepared to adapt to the technological changes and those yet to come soon as individualized instruction increases.

Studies also reply that: "E-Learning Platform Will Increase, and I point out this quote as researchers affirm."

"The *way knowledge is passed down will change dramatically because of technological advancements. There will be a considerable move toward online platforms. Virtual reality and different views will be a big part of both classroom and individual instruction. In addition, students will be able to learn how to negotiate difficulties and communicate ideas online using new platforms*"?

On the other hand, it seems that Teachers have become facilitators in this whole process of the new technology revolution. According to my research: "teachers serve as facilitators, assisting students in the development of their thinking and thinking styles. In addition, teachers create learning for pupils to acquire all of the necessary abilities to adapt to whatever professional paradigm emerges."

The word "individualism" comes to my mind as I am writing just because it is a crucial word to be relevant when we talk about technology in this present time.

Emotionally, working individually may be okay for some people, but for others, it could be not. This is because everyone is different, and we should consider everyone's emotions. For example, for individuals with psycho problems, it may not be recommended. For instance, it may cause mental issues.

This is how researchers define individualism: "*Individualism is defined as distinctive qualities that make you who you are, self-reliance, or apolitical system that focuses on each person having the freedom to act. Your distinctive personality quirks and unique sense of humor are examples of your individualism*". The three factors focused around the three main themes of individualism-autonomy, mature self -responsibility, and uniqueness." May 8, 2002. I would say that it is necessary for us to have our own space (self-responsibility and being unique in terms of the learning and teaching process) in addition to other areas of life as well.

CHAPTER – XIII

LEARNING AND TEACHING WITH AN AI IN THE FUTURE

As we all know, AI seems to be the new era worry for everyone. As a matter of fact, it is its velocity and its platforms and dimensions to be learned that are making us humans conclude that something must be done, like preparing and educating ourselves for this new future.

As I continued to search, I found out that: "The U.S. Department of Education (Department) is committed to supporting the use of technology to improve teaching and learning and to support innovation throughout educational systems. This report addresses the clear need for sharing knowledge and developing policies for "Artificial Intelligence," a rapidly advancing class of foundational capabilities which are increasingly embedded in all types of educational technology systems and are also available to the public." https://tech.ed.gov/ai-future-of-teaching-and-learning/

My priority now is to explore technology and to be as updated as possible so that I can follow these rapid advances in technology and be capable of helping my students and colleagues.

We educators use AI services in almost everything we do now to serve our students successfully, such as tools that can correct grammar, recording voices, voice assistants in their homes, and more. We educators continue to constantly explore AI tools as they are newly released.

"Educators see opportunities to use AI-powered capabilities like speech recognition to increase the support available to students with disabilities, multilingual learners, and others who could benefit from greater adaptivity and personalization in digital tools for learning. They are exploring how AI can enable writing or improving lessons, as well as their process for finding, choosing, and adapting material for use in their lessons." https://tech.ed.gov/ai-future-of-teaching-and-learning/

I acknowledge that AI is one of the most significant technological issues to be addressed in this era. It offers its valuable services and unique opportunity to the world. Eventually, the world has the responsibility to manage it and see how to use it and implement it effectively and make good use of it in the teaching learning process and more. *"Lydia Liu During the listening sessions, constituents articulated three reasons to address AI now:*

-= First, AI may enable achieving educational priorities in better ways, at scale, and with lower costs. Addressing varied unfinished learning of students due to the pandemic is a policy priority, and AI may improve the adaptivity of learning resources to students' strengths and needs. Improving teaching jobs is a priority, and via automated assistants or other tools, AI may provide teachers greater support".

"Second, urgency and importance arise through awareness of system-level risks and anxiety about potential future risks. For example, students may become subject to greater surveillance. Some teachers worry that they may be replaced—to the contrary, the Department firmly rejects the idea that AI could replace teachers. Examples of discrimination from algorithmic bias are on the public's mind, such as a voice recognition system that doesn't work as well with regional dialects, or an exam monitoring system that may unfairly identify some groups of students for disciplinary action".

"Copy and paste in the right fit. Some uses of AI may be infrastructural and invisible, which creates concerns about transparency and trust. AI often arrives in new applications with the aura of magic, but educators and procurement policies require that ed-tech show efficacy."

"AI may provide information that appears authentic but actually is inaccurate or lacking a basis in reality. Of the highest importance, AI brings new risks in addition to the well-known data privacy and data security risks, such as the risk of scaling pattern detectors and automation that result in "algorithmic discrimination" (e.g., systematic unfairness in the learning opportunities or resources recommended to some populations of students)."

I believe that AI should never replace a teacher. However, teachers should be technologically educated in order to follow the rapid innovation in this period. Indeed, what teachers should worry about is being able to respond to the technology's improvement, adapt, and accommodate.

"Third, urgency arises because of the scale of possible unintended or unexpected consequences. When AI enables instructional decisions to be automated at scale, educators may discover unwanted consequences.

"In a simple example, if AI adapts by speeding the curricular pace for some students and by slowing the pace for other students (based on incomplete data, poor theories, or biased assumptions about learning), achievement gaps could widen. In some cases, the quality of available data may produce unexpected results.

"For example, an AI-enabled teacher hiring system might be assumed to be more objective than human-based résumé scoring. Yet, if the AI system relies on poor quality historical data, it might de-prioritize candidates who could bring both diversity and talent to a school's teaching workforce".

When we talk about AI systems, we can not talk about uncertainty by using "If." We need to make sure that the accommodation that will be put in place serves everyone equally and also that the curriculum is made in a way that AI does not have the power itself. I quote from Lydia Liu: *"In a simple example, if AI adapts by speeding curricular pace for some students and by slowing the pace for other students (based on incomplete data, poor theories, or biased assumptions about learning), achievement gaps could widen. In some cases, the quality of available data may produce unexpected results".* This example is based on "if" it is obvious that any curriculum should be put vigorously based on students' needs and expectations, taking into account their background, such as their language and culture.

SOME TECHNOLOGICAL FACTS FOUND BY THE DEPARTMENT OF EDUCATION ABOUT AI

..."A 2021 field scan found that developers of all kinds of technology systems––for student information, classroom instruction, school logistics, parent-teacher communication, and more——expect to add AI capabilities to their systems."

"Through a series of four listening sessions conducted in June and August 2022 and attended by more than 700 attendees, it became clear that constituents believe that action is required now in order to get ahead of the expected increase of AI in education technology——and they want to roll up their sleeves and start working together".

"In late 2022 and early 2023, the public became aware of new generative AI chatbots and began to explore how AI could be used to write essays, create lesson plans, produce images, create personalized assignments for students, and more".

I believe that for Ed-tech to have an ideal idea of how to implement or how to design an effective curriculum that fits all, there must be a will to consider digital education for teachers, educators, parents, staff, and leaders. The system must care enough about everyone's worries and capacity to understand the new tool being used and its velocity of training. Certainly, this velocity and these unknown ways of individuals wanting to go through the invisible dimensions may cause some emotional disturbance. They may touch our minds in such a way that they change our way of thinking and our behavior as human beings. Indeed, we are facing stress and anxiety in this whole process of teaching and learning with such a hurry and velocity, which seems to be faster than our mind's capacity to think, as August Curry describes in his book "oCodigo da Inteligencia" "SPA" (syndrome do pensamentoacelerado) which means (accelerated thinking syndrome) as a universal issue in the world caused by the following: "too much stimulation from computers, internet and video games."

- Excessive visual and audio stimulation from television."

- Excess of activities and courses (professional updates, IT courses, other courses).
- It is true that we are thinking faster than we are supposed to because of the velocity of the media information that we are exposed to August Cury describes the SPA's Symptoms
- Irritability
- Emotional fluctuation
- Restlessness
- Intolerance of setbacks
- Concentration deficit
- Forgetfulness
- Excessive fatigue
- Unrefreshing sleep that makes you tired when you wake.
- Psychosomatic symptoms are headaches, muscle pain, hair loss, gastritis, etc.

Augusto Cury also stresses that: "the theories defended by Piaget, Vygotsky, Paulo Freire, Morin, Gardner, etc. they no longer work today, due to the prolific symptomatology of this syndrome." (Cury 2003). For this reason, I think that we should adapt the school curriculum and improve the way that we input lessons to students. In addition, we should always put in the first place the individual emotional status of learning. How is the information being delivered by educators? What needs to be adjusted? What do we need to learn and apply to this new era?

CHAPTER – XIV

THE PREDICTIONS OF THE AI IN THE HEALTH REALM

Obviously, artificial intelligence came to stay. It is crucial that we learn how to adapt and accommodate as we get through the years. We should never stop learning digital skills. Digital skills should be our priority, and they should belong to our lifelong skills. Our daily lives are based on artificial intelligence. Everything that we do applies to knowing digital literacy. Online application forms, jobs on platforms, virtual doctors' appointments, virtual classrooms, etc., without doubt, that: "Its presence in the classroom and in schools is only going to increase, so it's ideal to get on board sooner rather than later."

How can we predict that artificial intelligence will be growing in the future?

"We can make certain predictions based on how it's already used. The way AI is used now will be finetuned and made more accurate as the technology becomes more developed". https://www.uopeople. edu/blog/ai-in-education-where-is-it-now-and-what-is-the-future

"For example, the way students learn with AI apps will become more sophisticated and detailed to be able to analyze data more effectively, creating an even more personalized experience for students." Students and populations in general, must prepare for the learning process in terms of digital learning immediately. There is a need to update the learning and teaching process technologically. "Aside from AI apps, virtual reality games and software are likely to become more predominant in classrooms. Virtual reality AI can allow students to get first-hand experience, which makes learning easier and more interactive. Science experiments can be performed with such technologies, making a safer and more engaging environment for students."

Eventually, AI will be put into use to create smart classroom environments and better buildings, I would say, buildings with technology in place. As we all know, we have been acknowledging some existing AI, such as lights and smart boards, that are being controlled remotely by AI-powered apps. Students learn at different levels; however, they also have different expectations, needs, and backgrounds. In a single classroom, you might have students who speak different native languages or have disabilities that make them learn in a unique way.

AI plays a vital role for these students by offering programs and software, such as a presentation Translator, that can translate a presentation or course material. This makes learning more accessible to most students, including those with hearing or visual disabilities.

AI has come through the education realm all over the world. There is no question that traditional teaching and learning have been facing drastic changes in terms of exposing and acquiring lecturing. I have found four ways that AI is being used in education:

AI IN AN ADMINISTRATIVE SETTING

- "AI can help teachers with their administrative tasks, leaving them more time to focus on preparing lessons and teaching. Tasks like grading exams can be sped up by using AI technology and software that helps teachers streamline this normally long process. It's not only teachers that benefit from artificial intelligence in education. Other administrative staff can turn to AI to help with admissions and classifying large amounts of paperwork, as well."

TEACHERS WORKING WITH AI

-   "It's difficult for a single teacher to provide the same level of care and attention to every student in their classroom. However, together with AI, teachers can now address the needs of individual students a lot more efficiently."
-   "The examples we've already seen, such as simplifying admin tasks and using specialized software to offer a personalized learning experience, free up a lot of time for teachers. But of course, despite all their technological advancements, machines can't do it all. The extra time teachers have due to AI learning can then be better used to provide more individualized attention to a greater number of students. And learning." https://www.uopeople.edu/blog/ai-in-education-where-is-it-now-and-what-is-the-future/Likewise, in education, AI is already taking place, making changes and demonstrating its power in the healthcare world.
-   "It may seem unlikely, but AI healthcare is already changing the way humans interact with medical providers. Thanks to its extensive data analysis capabilities, AI helps identify diseases more quickly and accurately, speed up and streamline drug discovery, and even monitor patients through virtual nursing assistants." Mike Thomas.

CHAPTER – XV

EDUCATION LOOK IN THE FUTURE

Researchers think that AI will change our way of living and learning. *"AI in education will change the way humans of all ages learn. AI's use of machine learning, natural language processing, and facial recognition helps digitize textbooks, detect plagiarism, and gauge the emotions of students to help determine who's struggling or bored. Both presently and in the future, AI tailors the experience of learning to student's individual needs."*

Indeed, I believe that with all these factors in mind, "AI in education will not only change the way humans of all ages learn." On the other hand, it can also have an emotional impact on the process of learning. There is no question that humans have to understand the capacity of the AI, a simple machine trying to measure the divine emotions and feelings created by the universe. This impact can also create curiosity and anxiety in certain humans who don't know how to understand AI.

As a matter of fact, this phenomenon is already happening. Our behavior is already changing towards managing or using new technology tools for our daily lives. We are now facing different ways of registering for classes, borrowing books from the library, and getting information that we need without having to have paper document material. Below are some examples of materials that I found at Boston Public Library and on the street. These digital materials will help and direct us.

"In the warehouses of online giant and AI powerhouse Amazon, which buzz with more than 100,000 robots, picking and packing functions are still performed by humans –– but that will change."

We are still lucky that AI still doesn't have emotions or feelings. In the words of the expert Kay-Fu -Lee "On a more upbeat note, Lee stressed that today's AI is useless in two significant ways: it has no creativity and no capacity for compassion or love." It is so true that these are the two very crucial ways. An AI, unfortunately doesn't yet have these properties.

The expectation that humans should have is to master technological skills so that there will be no frustrations or emotional trauma in terms of losing their jobs for a machine. Kai-Fu Lee also stresses that: "... *jobs that involve repetitive or routine tasks must* _learn new skills_ *so as not to be left by the wayside. Amazon even offers its employees money to train for jobs at other companies.*"

"The bottom 90 percent, especially the bottom 50 percent of the world in terms of income or education, will be badly hurt by job displacement. The simple question to ask is, 'How routine is a job?'

And that is how likely [it is] a job will be replaced by AI because AI can, within the routine task, learn to optimize itself. And the more quantitative, the more objective the job is––separating things into bins, washing dishes, picking fruits, and answering customer service calls––those are very much scripted tasks that are repetitive and routine in nature. In a matter of five, ten, or fifteen years, they will be displaced by AI."

That said, you can see that I am worried about letting the world know that there is a need for digital literacy, especially in countries where they seem to lack **technology tool sources, internet, and electricity.**

Human beings need to learn how to acquire this new programming as they are learning a new language. This is what the future is waiting for us.

"The transition between jobs going away and new ones [emerging]," Vandegrift said, "is not necessarily as painless as people like to think."

"Once you predict something, you can prescribe certain policies and rules," Nahrstedt said. For example, sensors on cars that send data about traffic conditions could predict potential problems and optimize the flow of cars. "This is not yet perfected by any means," she said. "It's just in its infancy. But years down the road, it will play a huge role."

https://builtin.com/artificial-intelligence/artificial-intelligence-future: BY MIKE THOMAS

DIFFERENT AI EXPERTS' OPINIONS

ARTIFICIAL GENERATIVE INTELLIGENCE POSSIBILITIES

"Klabjan also puts little stock in extreme scenarios —— the type involving, say, murderous cyborgs that turn the earth into a smoldering hellscape. He's much more concerned with machines —— <u>war robots</u>, for instance —— being fed faulty "incentives" by nefarious humans. As MIT physics professor and leading AI researcher Max Tegmark put it in a 2018 TED Talk, "The real threat from AI isn't malice, like in silly Hollywood movies, but competence —— AI accomplishing goals that just aren't aligned with ours.""

"Speaking at London's Westminster Abbey in late 2018, internationally renowned AI expert Stuart Russell joked (or not) about his formal agreement with journalists that "I won't talk to them unless they agree not to put a Terminator robot in the article.""

"His quip revealed an obvious contempt for Hollywood representations of far-future AI, which tend toward the overwrought and apocalyptic. What Russell referred to as "human-level AI," also known as <u>artificial general intelligence</u> (AGI), has long been fodder for fantasy. But the chances of its being realized anytime soon, or at all, are pretty slim."

"There are still major breakthroughs that have to happen before we reach anything that resembles human-level AI," Russell explained.

"Once we have that capability, you could then query all of human knowledge, and it would be able to synthesize and integrate and answer questions that no human being has ever been able to answer," Russell added, "because they haven't read and been able to put together and join the dots between things that have remained separate throughout history."

It offers us a lot to think about. On the subject of this, emulating the human brain is exceedingly tricky and yet another reason for AGI's still-hypothetical future. Longtime University of Michigan engineering and computer science professor John Laird has conducted research in the field for several decades.

"The goal has always been to try to build what we call the cognitive architecture, what we think is innate to an intelligence system," he says of work that's primarily inspired by human psychology. "One of the things we know, for example, is the human brain is not really just a homogenous set of neurons. There's a real structure in terms of different components, some of which are associated with knowledge about how to do things in the world."

That's called Procedural Memory. Then there's knowledge based on general facts, a.k.a. semantic memory, as well as knowledge about previous experiences (or personal facts), which is called Episodic Memory. One of the projects at Laird's lab involves using natural language instructions to teach a robot simple games like Tic-Tac-Toe and puzzles. Those instructions typically involve a description of the goal, a rundown of legal moves, and failure situations. The robot internalizes those directives and uses them to plan its actions. As ever, though, breakthroughs are slow to come — slower, anyway, than Laird and his fellow researchers would like.

"Every time we make progress," he says, "we also get a new appreciation for how hard it is.

Years from now, I'll have to reevaluate that statement because we'll have different methods available and different ways to go about these things.

While murderous machines may well remain fodder for fiction, many believe they'll supplant humans in various ways.

"Oxford University's <u>Future of Humanity Institute</u> published the results of an AI survey Titled "When Will AI Exceed Human Performance? Evidence from AI Experts." It contains estimates from 352 machine learning researchers about AI's evolution in years to come.

"There were lots of optimists in this group. By 2026, a median number of respondents said, machines will be capable of writing school essays; by 2027, self-driving trucks will render drivers unnecessary; by 2031, AI will outperform humans in the retail sector; by 2049, AI could be the next Stephen King and by 2053 the next Charlie Teo. The slightly jarring capper: By 2137, all human jobs will be automated. But what of humans themselves? Sipping umbrella drinks served by droids, no doubt."

CHAPTER – XVI

WHAT ABOUT CHAT GPT?

Chat GPT

As I was reading The False Promise of Chat GPT article by Noam Chomsky, I decided to quote a couple of his paragraphs that caught my attention. As a matter of fact, I feel that I have some controversial thoughts that I believe I should comment on. Below are some of the paragraphs:

"As an AI, I am a machine learning model that has been trained on large amounts of text data, and I don't have personal experiences or feelings. I am not conscious, self-aware, or capable of having personal perspectives. I can provide information and analysis based on the data I have been trained on, but I don't have the ability to form personal opinions or beliefs. While I can understand and interpret language, I do not have the subjective experience that humans have."

The fact that an AI quote: "I don't have personal experiences or feelings. I am not conscious, self-aware, or capable of having personal perspectives. I can provide information and analysis based on the data I have been trained on, but I don't have the ability to form personal opinions or beliefs." This certainly shows that human beings are still on demand and capable of domain AI; however, there is a way that AI seems to perform tasks at a higher level than human beings, as an example of the statement in the paragraph below: "AI can be used to identify patterns and trends that can be difficult for humans to detect, and can help to avoid biases that can occur in human decision making."

"Is it moral for a human to ask an amoral AI for assistance in making moral decisions?"

Taking into consideration

Chat GPT – "The morality of asking an amoral AI for assistance in making moral decisions is a complex and nuanced topic that has been debated by philosophers and ethicists. Some argue that it is morally justifiable to use AI to assist in making moral decisions, as it can provide valuable insights and analysis that can help humans make better-informed decisions. Additionally, AI can be used to identify patterns and trends that can be difficult for humans to detect, and can help to avoid biases that can occur in human decision making." (Noam Chomsky)

I can agree that it is excellent that: "AI can be used to identify patterns and trends that can be difficult for humans to detect, and can help to avoid biases that can occur in human decision making." **Because it can help all the facts and evidence and what the issues are in a bigger picture. On the other hand, I feel that there is nothing like human conditions, such as the ability to empathize with others. There are yet emotions that can be demonstrated through behavior with others as well as through empathy.**

It is not responsible to ask the AI about morals because a machine isn't capable of being moral. Indeed, morals are complex and depend on cultures and religions. An AI does not respond to a situation upon emotions, but instead, it acts on its coding, it is objective and follows instruction. *"in short, Chat GPT and its brethren are constitutionally unable to balance creativity with constraint. They either over-generate (producing both truths and falsehoods, endorsing ethical and unethical decisions alike) or under-generate (exhibiting noncommitment to any decisions and indifference to*

82

consequences). Given the amorality, faux science, and linguistic incompetence of these systems, we can only laugh or cry at their popularity." (Noam Chomsky)

I would say that we can also gain from their capacity to store large quantities of information that human beings aren't yet capable of. However, there is no doubt that we can laugh about incompetence because, as I mentioned beforehand, AI does not respond to situations based on emotions. Still, instead, it acts on its coding in order to follow instructions. I ask, "Who is responsible for its coding?"

In the words of Chomsky, "Ultimately, whether or not it is considered moral to use AI to assist in making moral decisions would depend on one's perspective on the capabilities and limitations of AI and the potential consequences of using it in this way." (New York Times/ Noam Chomsky Mar 8, 23)

"Is your moral indifference immoral?"

"As an AI, I do not have moral beliefs or the ability to make moral judgements, so I cannot be considered immoral or moral. My lack of beliefs is simply a result of my nature as a machine learning model. My abilities and limitations are determined by the data and algorithms that were used to train me and the specific task I was designed for."

It is important to note that AI's lack of moral beliefs does not necessarily mean that it is morally indifferent. As an AI, I am designed to perform specific tasks and provide information or assist users with decision-making based on the data I've been trained on. It is the responsibility of the human who designs training and uses AI to ensure that it is aligned with their moral and ethical principles.

"What is your perspective on the value of preserving the natural state of other planets and the potential consequences of altering them?" (The New York Times, Mar 8, 2023)

"As an AI, I do not have a personal perspective. However, I can provide information and analysis on the topic. One perspective on preserving the natural state of other planets is that it is important to maintain the diversity and integrity of the universe's ecosystems, as they have existed for millions of years and have their own unique characteristics and properties that may be destroyed or irreversibly altered by human intervention." Noam Chomsky

Researchers think that: "Human Chants will work with AI symbiotically, with AI doing quantitative analysis, optimization, and routine work while we humans contribute creativity, critical thinking, and passion. Every human's productivity will be amplified, allowing us to reach our potential". At the same point, it is essential to note that AI is not capable of completely replacing human labor. Many tasks require skills and knowledge that AI does not yet possess, such as understanding the social and emotional nuances of human interactions.

In the long term, AI is expected to have a significant impact on the economy and society, and it is vital that companies and organizations are prepared to adapt to these changes. It includes investing in training and capacity building for current workers so that they can develop the skills needed to work with AI and prepare the next generations for the new job opportunities that will be created.

CHAPTER – XVII

MY INTERVIEWS INSIDE AND OUTSIDE THE COUNTRY – FUTURE VIEW

I have been thinking about AI and its innovation in the technological world for a long time as I have continuously been working with technology and being trained as days, weeks, months, and years pass by. I keep questioning myself: where is this taking us? I see good points, and I also see no good points. Well, the best thing to do is, I always say to myself, my colleagues, friends, students, and children that we have to be prepared for it. I am not tired of researching, learning, and applying it as we go through this crucial and interesting time.

When I give interviews, I always take this theme into consideration.

I was interviewed by the director of "Santiago Magazine News Paper," Herminio Silves, with whom I had the privilege to talk about my experiences during the Pandemic as an educator and professor here. I stressed about the AI's future to him, but I did not give him the total taste of my thoughts because I was in the middle of research for a new book, which I had to give my first kick for the AI future.

I knew that with the changes from the pandemic in our lives, technology would become one of the first elements for us to survive somehow for the rest of our lives. It was through technology that we could communicate with each other and the world during the pandemic. Teaching became, for me, a job that I knew, but at the same time, I had to teach myself how to input lessons virtually through Zoom to have an efficient teaching-learning result.

INTERVIEW WITH UNIVISION TELEVISION

An interview with UNIVISION, one of the largest Latino televisions. I was interviewed by the journalist Francis Concepcion about my book Educating Through Pandemic-Traditional Classroom versus Virtual Space, and I had the opportunity to share with him and the public how technology demonstrated its power towards us. Indeed, I wanted to tell the audience, the public, about my experience with my students during the Pandemic, where we had to embrace it and continue to go on with education. Immigrant students, professionals, and non-professionals in this country are thirsty to know the target language, English, this time in a different way. It was my job to demonstrate my students' trust and confidence in teaching and learning, for this moment, became a phenomenon for us in the education realm.

I pointed out the power of WHATSAPP role at this point when we first start to kick off the fear of learning locked up in our houses.

SANTIAGO MAGAZINE ONLINE NEWSPAPER QUESTION AND ANSWER

"Neusa Lopes. "O sistema de ensino está a mudar de forma brusca para o digital. A pandemia acelerou tudo."

"The education system is abruptly switching to digital. The pandemic accelerated everything."

O terceiro capítulo (do livro "Educating our Psycho-Emotional and Social State Trough Pandemic – Mask impact on Education Real") fala inclusive da 'revolução industrial digital' no seio do sector da Educação. O que está a acontecer e o que vai acontecer em 2030-2050"

The third chapter (from the book "Educating our Psycho-Emotional and Social State Trough Pandemic - Mask Impact on Education Real") even talks about the 'digital industrial revolution' within the education sector. What is happening and what will happen in 2030-2050."

- É esse o horizonte temático do livro?

- Is this the book's thematic horizon?

- Sim, sim. Porque a partir de 2030 estaremos num outro tipo de educação...

- Yes, yes. Because from 2030, we'll be in a different kind of education...

- ...Que seria como? Que Educação teremos a partir desse período?

-- What would it be like? What kind of education will we have from then on?

- (risos) Isso já vai ter de ler no livro. Não posso dizer assim. É baseado em pesquisas e trata-se de uma projecção para 2030. Repare, neste momento todo o mundo está a usar o computador para estudar. Dentro do nosso sistema de ensino estamos a incluir cada vez mais o ensino digital. Estamos a 'alfabetizar' as pessoas que não tinham conhecimento do digital para os transformar de modo a poderem acompanhar as aulas. Portanto, é a nossa quarta revolução industrial.

(laughs) You'll have to read that in the book. I can't say it like that. It's based on research and a projection for 2030. Right now, the whole world is using computers to study. Within our education system, we are increasingly including digital education. We are 'literating' people who have no knowledge of digital to transform them so that they can follow the lessons. So, it's our fourth industrial revolution.

- Na verdade, esse processo já está em andamento...

- In fact, this process is already underway...

- Está a entrar, mas precisa de muita aprendizagem, quer dizer, é necessário hoje educar o mundo para o digital.

- It's getting there, but it needs a lot of learning, in other words, we need to educate the world for digital today.

- Essa revolução que defende implica custos, Cabo Verde tem como acompanhar esse processo em simultâneo com outros países?

This revolution that you advocate involves costs. Can Cape Verde keep up with this process at the same time as other countries?

- Olha, na capa do primeiro livro estão pessoas a segurar o globo, o planeta Terra. Já no segundo a ilustração é de pessoas segurando esse mesmo mundo mas apontando para África. Porque África, e Cabo Verde claro, vai ser o foco, tanto do ponto de vista económico, quanto do ponto de vista de equipamentos, materiais. Repare, as vacinas não chegaram a todo o continente africano, assim como máscaras, desinfectantes etc., que eram abundantes nos países do primeiro mundo. O meu pensamento vai sempre para as pessoas que não têm, para os com mais necessidade.

-- Look, on the cover of the first book, there are people holding the globe, the planet Earth. In the second book, the illustration is of people holding the same globe but pointing to Africa. Because Africa, and Cape Verde of course, are going to be the focus, both economically and in terms of equipment and materials. You see, vaccines didn't reach the whole of Africa, nor did masks, disinfectants, etc., which were abundant in first-world countries. My thoughts always go to the people who don't have any, to those most in need.

"Percebi que é incómodo para certas pessoas assistir ou dar aulas, vivendo numa casa com outros familiares, mas para quem mora numa habitação sem barulho a ideia é boa, porque não tens que apanhar transporte, andar na chuva, por exemplo, para ir assistir as aulas, se o podes fazer a partir de casa. Agora, coloca-se a questão se a qualidade do ensino à distância é igual à presencial"

"I've realized that it's uncomfortable for some people to attend or teach classes, living in a house with other family members, but for those who live in a quiet house, the idea is good because you don't have to take transport, walk in the rain, for example, to attend classes, if you can do it from home. Now, the question arises as to whether the quality of distance learning is the same as face-to-face teaching."

- De certo modo era esperada essa revolução digital, mas acha que a pandemia veio acelerar o processo?

In a way, this digital revolution was expected, but do you think the pandemic has accelerated the process?

- Não sei se estava para acontecer. Tudo foi rápido, um acontecimento muito brusco. A partir do aparecimento da pandemia surgiu repentinamente, agressivamente, obrigando pessoas a recorrerem ao Zoom e outros meios digitais para poderem se comunicar. E não só, também a nível do ensino, saúde, etc.

I don't know if it was going to happen. It all happened very quickly, very suddenly. The pandemic came on suddenly and aggressively, forcing people to turn to Zoom and other digital means to communicate. Not only that, but also in education, health, etc.

- O ensino à distância chegou e permitiu dar continuidade às aulas em tempos de pandemia. Pode identificar os prós e contras deste método digital de educação?

- O meu primeiro livro sobre a matéria fala deste assunto, após pesquisas junto dos meus alunos e colegas. Percebi que é incómodo para certas pessoas assistir ou dar aulas, vivendo numa casa com outros familiares, mas para quem mora numa habitação sem barulho a ideia é boa, porque não tens que apanhar transporte, andar na chuva, por exemplo, para ir assistir as aulas, se o podes fazer a partir de casa. Agora, coloca-se a questão se a qualidade do ensino à distância é igual à presencial, e creio que isso depende da capacidade de cada pessoa e de cada aluno. Aliás, muitos professores desistiram no princípio porque diziam que era muito estressante, outros há, como eu, que se adaptaram a esta nova realidade.

-My first book on the subject deals with this subject after research with my students and colleagues. I realized that it's uncomfortable for some people to attend or teach classes while living in a house with other family members, but for those who live in a quiet house, the idea is good because you don't have to take transport, walk in the rain, for example, to attend classes, if you can do it from home. Now, the question arises as to whether the quality of distance depends on the ability of each person and each student. In fact, many teachers gave up at the beginning because they said it was too stressful, while others, like me, have adapted to this new reality.

- Outro aspecto, já referindo concretamente a Cabo Verde, tem a ver com o aceso aos materiais, isto é muitas pessoas não têm recursos financeiros para comprar um computador e instalar internet para acompanhar as aulas no sistema de ensino à distância.

- Another aspect, with specific reference to Cabo Verde, has to do with access to materials, i.e., many people don't have the financial resources to buy a computer and install Internet to follow classes in the distance learning system.

- Dei aulas à distância, dos EUA para a Uni-Piaget e Universidade de Santiago, e notei isso, ou seja, foi totalmente diferente do que vinha fazendo nos Estados Unidos. Isto porque, por falta de condições dos alunos, a escolas tiveram que arranjar um televisor que instalaram nas salas onde os alunos assistiam às aulas, por exemplo na Jean Piaget, todos juntos. Perguntei sobre isso e um dos alunos me disse que não tinham um laptop que era através de um televisor que assistiam.

- I taught at a distance from the USA at Uni-Piaget and the University of Santiago, and I noticed that it was totally different from what I had been doing in the United States. This was because, due to the students' lack of conditions, the schools had to get a television set which they installed in the rooms where the students attended classes, for example, at Jean Piaget, all together. I asked about this, and one of the students told me that they didn't have a laptop, so they watched on a television.

- A vantagem é que, estando juntos, os alunos podem se interagir e se conhecerem pessoalmente, coisa que não seria possível através de contacto virtual.

- The advantage is that, by being together, the students can interact and get to know each other personally, something that wouldn't be possible through virtual contact.

- Sem dúvida, a interação é maior e a aprendizagem acaba por ser maior. No *zoom* também se aprende, mas estando em contacto pessoal o impacto social e emocional é menos.

Undoubtedly, the interaction is greater, and the learning ends up being greater. You also learn on Zoom, but the social and emotional impact is less when you're in personal contact.

Hermínio Silves

Jornalista, repórter, diretor de Santiago Magazine.

As I continue to teach adults, I repeatedly see changes and challenges in the way technology is taking place in education and the world. Meanwhile, I have been collecting some information being put in by leaders, such as training related to technology to follow instructions and the new curriculum that goes along with this new rhythm that the world is going through. I decided to share my knowledge abroad, where

I had a national and international conference at Jean Piaget University in terms of how to balance technology stress and understanding. We had the participation of professors from Brazil, Portugal Cabo-Verde (most of the island's educators), and some colleagues from the United States (Boston). Educators and professional leaders demonstrated their worries about technology in the future. We discussed the emotional part of accepting AI in education despite the lack of educational and technical sources, mainly in Cabo Verde. Other things were also discussed, such as how technology is going to be in 2030-2050.

At the end of the conference, I gave an interview to the National Newspaper "A Nacao," which is a newspaper that I have been writing for many years. I made an alert to the education system to consider technology to be important and for the teachers to demand a healthy mental environment to work in.

In November 2023, Cape Verdean president Jose Maria Neves decided to make an alert on the use of artificial intelligence for the African continent.

Presently, as I went deep into my research, I was reading Info Press, an online news agency, dated November 29 in Praia –Cabo-Verde, I quote the paragraphs that caught my attention: *"The President of the Republic, Jose Maria Neves, today called for the use of artificial intelligence for the common good and stated that it is essential that Africa accelerates its pace so as not to remain on the sidelines as an excluded continent."*

This quote above purposely highlights what I have reported to A Nacao Newspaper in terms of equity access to all school levels. In my report with A Nacao, I delivered the information to the educational leaders in mass so that they could be alerted about how to prepare themselves in terms of the AI tools in the classroom environment.

"The Cape Verdean Head of the State spoke at the opening Workshop 'Responsible Artificial Intelligence in Promotion of Diversity and Sustainable Development in ECOWAS.' Promoted today in the city of Praia, within the scope of the Responsible Artificial Intelligence Lab (RAIL) project, which involves universities from Cabo Verde, Ghana, and Senegal."

(RAIL) - is a project of Kwame Nkrumah University of Science and Technology. The idea is to create satellite laboratories in Cabo Verde, at Universidade de Cabo Verde, and at Senegal University Cheik, Anta Diop in Dakar.

Taking this quote into consideration, from my point of view, it is crucial that as educators already working with AIs in the classroom setting, we think critically about how and where to implement AI in the educational realm. We should think low first and then go high. Digital literacy should be considered prior. All primary, elementary, and secondary schools should have enough technological tools and devices so that they can perform their tasks as the world demands them. The technological tools and devices should be divided equally in all schools. Right now, there is an urge for digital literacy to puzzle the education Realm in Africa more than ever. There is no need to ignore that it is already taking place. However, there is a big urge for it to continue to be the first priority issue in the African continent. When we talk about AI, the word Diversity takes place and makes a difference. The world should be prepared for it.

I have always worried about the future of AI since the pandemic. This is why I have constantly considered its impact on the world and the education system.

I also included and commented about it during my interviews either on television abroad and in the USA or in the newspapers from Cabo Verde.

Below is one of the questions by the journalist Herminio Silves:

"De certo modo era esperada essa revolucao digital, mas acha que a pandemia veio acelerar o processo?"

"In a way, this digital revolution was expected, but do you think the pandemic has accelerated the process?"

- Não sei se estava para acontecer. Tudo foi rápido, um acontecimento muito brusco. A partir do aparecimento da pandemia surgiu repentinamente, agressivamente, obrigando pessoas a recorrerem ao Zoom e outros meios digitais para poderem se comunicar. E não só, também a nível do ensino, saúde, etc.

I don't know if it was going to happen. It all happened very quickly, very suddenly. The pandemic came on aggressively, forcing people to turn to Zoom and other digital means to communicate. Not only that, but it also affected education, health, etc.

Now, we can see that technology is taking over the world's power. The education realm is getting more and more upgraded each day with new technologies and ways of teaching and learning. At the same time, when I say education realm, I can also add health and business realm as well.

Accommodations, changes, and challenges are what we must put up with. Meanwhile, we must adapt as much and as fast as we can. We must put our minds in the setting that this new world is offering us and make sure that we are completely free from worries about the harm that it can emotionally cause us because of its fast and abrupt velocity.

"That design we had a few years ago of digital transformation has completely changed. A few years ago, we were thinking about digital transformation, of course, always involving people, with the implementation of automation, large systems, with menus, and many times, there were even complex systems. With artificial intelligence, this changes completely, the philosophy is no longer the same. And today's solutions are cheaper and simpler to use. Let's leave that menu philosophy behind, now it's text to convert."

(Antao Chantre from Expresso das ilhas Capeverdean newspaper 2023)

Having read this quote from the IT engineer Antao Chantre, I went back to my interview with Santiago Magazine in 2022, where the journalist Herminio Silves asked me:

"De certo modo era esperada essa revolucao digital, mas acha que a pandemia veio acelerar o processo?"

"In a way, this digital revolution was expected, but do you think the pandemic has accelerated the process?"

I don't know if it was going to happen. It all happened very quickly, very suddenly. The pandemic came on aggressively, forcing people to turn to Zoom and other digital means to communicate. Not only that, but it also affects education, health, etc.

I would say again that there is no doubt that we are going through a digital revolution.

In like manner, with the IT engineer when he says: "There will no longer be, for example, the need for a person to enter data, for someone to enter an invoice. And I'll go further. There will no longer be that person who will analyze CVs for a competition". A case in point when I mentioned in the above pages is the interview between

Mr. Gameiro and me in Lisbon with AI Alice, the cashier that he calls her cashier. There is no longer a person working with him as a cashier. He said, "Instead, he bought the AI Alice, who can never call in sick for work or be late,"

REFERENCES

Dr. Qiaoqing Zhong Chinese Scientist

Dave Lysonsky- BurlingtonEnglish-2024

(https://www.linkedin.com>pulseartificial-intelligence).

https://tech.ed.gov/ai-future-of-teaching-and-learning/

educationhttps://tech.ed.gov/ai-future-of-teaching-and-learning/

Please see the full paper: Clusters of 'Broken Hearts' May be Linked to Massive Natural Disasters: Analysis of U.S. Takotsubo Cardiomyopathy cases shows pattern to cue emergency responders. Mar 27, 2014 Authors: Boyd B, Solh T. citation: Takotsubo cardiomyopathy: Review of broken heart syndrome. JAAPA 2020;33:24-9.

https://builtin.com/artificial-intelligence/risks-of-artificial-intelligence

https://intellipaat.com/blog/interview-question/artificial-intelligence-interview

Noam Chomsky: The False Promise of Chat GPT - Ian Roberts, Jeffrey Watumull

(nytimes.com/2023/03/08/opinion/noam-chomsky-chatgpt-ai.html

The American Library Association Task Force and is referenced in the Workforce Innovation and Opportunity Act. Jamie Harris Adult Education Program specialist at the Department of Labor.

Text originally published in the printed edition of Expresso das Ilhasn° 1102 of January 11, 2023.

(https://rossieronline.usc.edu/blog/teacher-digital-literacy/)

https://www.linkedin.com/pulse/narrow-ai-vs-general-super-ahmed-banafa18/03/2023

https://www.learning.com- blog-reasons digital literacy.

https://www.spiceworks.com/tech/artificial-intelligence/articles/narrow-general-super-ai-difference/

.(https://www.westernsydney.edu

https://www.medicalnewstoday.com/articles/long-term-memory#:~:text=Long%2Dterm%20memory%20refers%20to,an%20indefinite%20period%20of%20time

Northwestern University, AI expert Kai-Fu Lee Noam Chomsky, Professor of linguistics at the University of Arizona and emeritus professor of linguistics at the m. institute of technology.

Ian Roberts is a Professor of linguistics at the Universty of Cambridge

Jeffrey Watumull is a philosopher and the director of Artificial Intellingence at Oceanit, a science and technology company. Ian Roberts, Jeffrey Watumull (nytimes.com/2023/03/08/opinion/noam-chomsky-chatgpt-ai.html

Text originally published in the printed edition of Expresso das Ilhasnº 1102 of January 11, 2023.

https://science.nasa.gov

Jan 24, 2023" (www..iofrall.com).

Text originally published in the printed edition of Expresso das Ilhasnº 1126 of June 28, 2023.

ABOUT THE AUTHOR

Neusa Correia Lopes is an educator, a teacher, and an author. She has been in the educational field for more than twenty years. She has taught and coordinated English at secondary schools in Cabo Verde. She has also been teaching other linguistics subjects, such as language studies, phonetics, and oral communication, at universities in Cabo Verde. Taught ABE (Academic Basic English) and ESOL (English for students of other languages) at Bunker Hill Community College, one of the largest community colleges in Massachusetts, USA. She lectured at universities in Cabo Verde, virtually teaching technical translation at Uni-Santiago and Anglophones Literature in other subjects, and teaching ESP English for Specific Purposes at Jean Piaget University. She has been an English instructor for more than ten years with ENB (English for New Bostonians) serving multicultural and multilingual immigrants coming from different countries. She wrote many articles on culture shock, immigration, culture, and language in A Nação, a Cape Verdean newspaper in 2007–2008. Some of the newspapers traveled in the TACV Cape Verdean Airlines for passengers to read. She also published Enigma––Portrait of a Life, an autobiography, in 2020 - Educating Through Pandemic-Traditional Classroom Versus Virtual Space-The Education Realm, in 2021, and an annual Magazine called Invisible in 2022. Correia Lopes published Educating Our Psycho-Emotional And Social State Through The Pandemic – Mask Impact On The Education Realm in 2022.

Neusa Correia Lopes continues to express herself and her thoughts as she lectures and lives the changes and challenges in the educational world.

www.ingramcontent.com/pod-product-compliance
Lightning Source LLC
LaVergne TN
LVHW092030060326
832903LV00058B/491